The emotional experience of learning and teaching

Routledge Education Books

Advisory editor: John Eggleston
Professor of Education
University of Keele

The emotional experience of learning and teaching

Isca Salzberger-Wittenberg
Gianna Henry
Elsie Osborne

Routledge & Kegan Paul
London, Boston, Melbourne and Henley

First published in 1983
by Routledge & Kegan Paul plc
39 Store Street, London WC1E 7DD,
9 Park Street, Boston, Mass. 02108, USA,
296 Beaconsfield Parade, Middle Park,
Melbourne, 3206, Australia
and Broadway House, Newtown Road,
Henley-on-Thames, Oxon RG9 1EN
Printed in Great Britain by
The Thetford Press Ltd, Thetford, Norfolk

Library of Congress Cataloging in Publication Data

Salzberger-Wittenberg, Isca.

The emotional experience of learning and teaching.
(Routledge education books)
Bibliography: p.
1. Learning. 2. Teacher-student relationships.
3. Interaction analysis in education. 4. Parent-teacher
relationships. I. Henry, Gianna. II. Osborne, Elsie L.
(Elsie Letitia) III. Title. IV. Series.
LB1060.S24 1983   371.1'02   83-3140

ISBN 0-7100-9511-2 (pbk.)

Contents

Contents

Contents

Introduction

This book aims to heighten the awareness of the emotional factors which enter into the process of learning and teaching. A better understanding of the nature of the interaction between student and teacher may help both to work towards a more fruitful relationship.

We learn about the world and ourselves from the moment we are born and continue to do so throughout our lives. Our learning, in infancy and for a considerable period, takes place within a dependent relationship to another human being. It is the quality of this relationship which deeply influences the hopefulness required to remain curious and open to new experiences, the capacity to perceive connections and to discover their meaning. Effective and cognitive aspects of learning are therefore closely linked and inter-dependent.

The book does not set out to give a systematic outline of the development of the individual, nor is it a sociological study. Instead it takes as its starting point the ordinary situations in which students and teachers find themselves and examines what these experiences mean to the individuals engaged in them. It attempts to throw light on the intra-psychic and intra-personal factors which enter into learning, the relationship of the student to the teacher, and the teacher's relationship to the student. In the rush of activities within an educational institution, there is little time and space to reflect on the meaning of the interactions that take place. It is hoped that the book will provide food for thought for teachers, whether in infant, primary, secondary or tertiary education, to help them to observe the phenomena they encounter, to think about them and make sense of them.

In infant and primary schools attention is usually given to the emotional needs of children and the requirements of any particular child. Some teachers, however, are eager to 'take over' from the parents, considering themselves better equipped to understand and provide for the child. It is important that they see themselves as bridge-builders between home and school. They are in fact facilitators of a delicate transition, helping the child to extend his relationship from within the family to those with teachers and with children of the same age group. They lay the foundation of the child's relationship to teaching staff, to learning within a group and becoming part of an educational establishment.

Some of these children will go on to schools which concentrate on the academic side of learning. Some teachers are puzzled by the fact that, in spite of good teaching and high intelligence, their pupils do not succeed. When children are bright it is easy to overlook the emotional difficulties that beset them. They may be the object of considerable pressure to live up to the expectations placed upon them by parents and teachers. Their fear of letting down their elders may interfere with, rather than promote, their achievement. On the other hand, their failure may be a way of showing their resentment at being fitted into an emotional strait-jacket.

Many teachers in less privileged secondary schools have to contend with large classes and exceedingly big institutions. They find themselves weighed down and overwhelmed by the difficult children and difficult situations they encounter. In order to escape from this burden, they attempt to find quick and forceful ways of managing. Although such measures may sometimes be effective in the short run, they are often detrimental to their own and their students' development. Conflicting pressure and stress leads many teachers to wish to shut themselves off altogether from the awareness of their students' suffering. Others become worried and despairing about the wasting away of the creative potential of the children and young people in their care. The result is that quite a few teachers find little satisfaction in their work. Some lose their self-respect or give up teaching altogether. Yet many of these same teachers will have entered the profession with high ideals, wishing to provide an education and an environment for youngsters that will enable them to grow and mature into creative adults.

Teachers involved in tertiary education are often puzzled and appalled by the extent of the personal problems of their students. Because they do not fully understand the nature of the difficulties, they tend to become over-involved, or to be merely critical or avoid facing them. Teachers of mature adults are surprised that learning and the learning relationship to the staff evokes attitudes which they are inclined to associate with children and adolescents.

Thus teachers of all age groups find themselves puzzled, concerned or worried about their pupils. This book offers no easy answers. It does, however, show that detailed observation and awareness of verbal and non-verbal communications can provide us with information about the nature of the problem and thus lead to a more constructive approach to it. The book is based on the work done by the authors with a group of teachers who attended the Tavistock Clinic for a course called Aspects of

Counselling in Education. Although the staff of the Tavistock have some experience of teaching, our particular expertise derives from close attention to the emotional states as they are revealed within the consulting room, as well as from direct observation of infants and young children in their own homes and schools. Our wish to communicate the insights we have gained stems from the conviction that: (a) they are of particular relevance to the field of education, and (b) that teachers play a very important part in the life of young people; they provide a framework which either assists or hinders emotional and mental growth. Teachers themselves tend to either overrate or underrate the part they play in the development of their pupils. Those who overrate their role, deny the importance of the parents, while others are convinced that all emotional and behavioural difficulties are due to inheritance and/or an unsatisfactory home background. While this is true to some extent, the latter view underestimates the opportunity that the school and the teacher has for giving children a second chance to form relationships of a kind that may provide a sounder basis for their future.

Some educationalists feel that emotional problems are the province of specialists, like counsellors or clinicians. Specialist services serve a useful function in helping those who have difficulties which are beyond the expertise of teachers. However, educational institutions will have to continue to care for difficult children, and there are many parents who would never agree to seek psychological help outside the school. Those educational institutions who consider that caring for individuals should not be their concern, ignore their responsibility to consider whether the system itself or the relationship of any particular teacher to the student tends to foster growth, hinder it, or even promote casualties. Fortunately most teachers see themselves as being concerned with the whole person rather than simply the intellect of the pupil, and equally many schools and colleges feel it to be their function to promote education in its widest sense. They recognise that even the imparting of knowledge and social skills is highly dependent on the nature of the relationship between student and teacher, the individual and his fellow students, and the student and the institution as a whole.

The book has been conceived of as a whole and is most profitably read in sequence. Parts I, II and V have as their starting point the experiences with a large group of teacher-learners as I encountered them. I go on to outline concepts which may help us to think about the nature of the complex phenomena and show how understanding derived from insight can be applied in similar learning-teaching situations. The theoretical framework is psycho-analytic. Part III, contributed by Mrs Gianna Henry, is based on cases which the teachers brought for discussion. It shows how reflecting on the student's behaviour and one's own reactions to it can lead to understanding the nature of the relationship; this in turn can help the teacher to behave in a way that is likely to promote development. Part IV, contributed by Mrs Elsie Osborne, takes the application of insights into the field of work with the student's parents and with professional colleagues.

It will be evident that we are indebted to many teachers for helping us to learn about the problems in the learning-teaching relationship. In order to protect confidentiality, both that of the students and the educational institutions they attended, we shall not mention anyone by name. In as far as names occur in the text they are fictitious. We would, however, like to express our deep gratitude to those whose case material we have used, and indeed to all the teachers who participated in our courses and hence helped to contribute to this book.

Isca Salzberger-Wittenberg
Tavistock Clinic, London

Part I

Beginnings
I. Salzberger-Wittenberg

Chapter 1

Hopeful and fearful expectations

A new year, a new job, a new baby; the beginning of a new relationship, a book, a course of study – eagerly we turn to each new event with expectant hope. Untried, unsullied, it holds the promise of meeting some need as yet unmet, the fulfilment of desires as yet unfulfilled, the ideal we have never given up searching for. Unless, of course, past disillusionment has blunted our capacity for hope, made us fearful of risking disappointment yet again. But, however hopeful our anticipation, we also harbour fears about the future. 'Aller Anfang ist schwer' (every beginning is hard) says the wise German proverb, pointing to the uncertainty and doubts which tend to beset us. Will the new job be a failure, the course worthless, the new year bring disease and death, the journey end in disaster, the new baby be a monster? And in a less extreme vein: will they bring the same frustrations and difficulties that we have encountered before and had hoped to escape from? It is of the nature of beginning that the path ahead is unknown, leaving us poised as we enter upon it between wondrous excitement and anxious dread.

As I begin to write this book, I am filled with some degree of expectant hope; yet I am mainly burdened by the weightiness of the task that lies ahead. Empty pages face me as my mind is alternately a blank and in a state of chaos. Will, out of this uncertainty and confusion, any thoughts emerge, ideas be clothed into meaningful phrases, will they form themselves into some order? Do I have anything worthwhile to contribute? But as I reflect upon this despair, I become aware that these doubts and agonies are part and parcel of beginning, are the essence of any creative work. And then a somewhat reassuring thought occurs: 'I do have a basis in experience, something to start this chapter with.' I have recently been confronted with a group of teaching staff from primary, secondary and tertiary education beginnning a course at the Tavistock on Aspects of Counselling in Education.

A group of fifty strangers faced me this month at the start of the academic year. Lots of them sat bunched at the back, few had the courage to occupy the front rows. Someone arrived late noisily pushing past with a large shopping basket and was met by disapproving glances from those who h..d come on time. Some late-comers edged their way in shyly, attempting not to be noticed, while others apologised profusely. I was conscious of these happenings as I gave my introductory talk on the aims of the course. But I became increasingly aware of the tenseness of the people in front of me, the cursory glances around the room, faces turned towards me without appearing to comprehend. So I gave up the pursuit of my lecture and took hold of the moment. It occurred to me that as the course is intended to heighten awareness of what students and teachers feel in their respective situations, perhaps this aim would be best served if we started in the here and now, considering what it is like to enter a strange building, meet a group of strangers, begin a course. I took a risk and asked the group to comment on what they felt like, but to my relief they were keen enough to meet the challenge, after I had explained that I had no wish to intrude on their privacy but hoped that reflecting upon their own experiences would be a useful way of learning about such matters.

'I felt embarrassed coming in late, I thought you might be angry,' said one.

'I thought that there was no chair left for me, that would have been the last straw,' said another. Soon others expressed their feelings:

'I feel lost and confused.' 'So do I; the receptionist told me where to go but I twice opened the wrong door, this is such a big and frightening place.'

'I was relieved when you entered and took control, I thought being in a large group without a leader was frightening.'

'One does not know what is expected of one, so one waits for others to say something.'

'I feel exposed.'

'I have been teaching for many years, I'm afraid I'll find out that I have had the wrong ideas about children, that the course will shake my beliefs.'

'I feel ignorant and stupid and I wonder why I have been chosen. How do you select people for this course?'

'One feels so alone amongst strangers, I was looking around to see if there might be someone I know.'

'I feel isolated and want to be near someone for comfort – did you put the chairs close together for that reason?'

'When I read the printed information sheet, I felt it implied some secret authority watching one.'

'I wonder what rules and controls you have here?'

'I wonder what's hidden behind the door.'

'I don't know what you are all talking about, I am just keen and interested.'

'When I first came in, I thought how cold and dull this place was – I find it brighter now.'

Does it seem surprising that these statements were made, not by young children, not by 18-year-old college students, but by a group of senior teaching staff who found themselves at the beginning of a new experience. Nor was this group in any way unusual, except in their willingness to scrutinise their feelings and their honesty in reporting the findings. Of course, everyone knows about feelings of insecurity, but we tend to pay lip-service to these, hide them, ignore them or ride rough-shod over them. Certainly, our group of teachers was amazed at the acuteness and intensity of their experience. We realised that the anxieties were far more numerous and powerful at the beginning yet, having verbally expressed and shared these, there was a more positive feeling that the situation wasn't perhaps as bad as all that. For the acknowledgment of fears leads us to test them against reality, allows us to bring them within the surveyance of the more mature part of the personality. Instead of being overwhelmed or denying their existence, we can recognise them as a legitimate part of ourselves and utilise our adult capabilities to deal with the situation.

The purpose of engaging the teachers in such scrutinisation of their here and now experience was neither a therapeutic one nor a model setting intended to be used in school situations. It simply provided an opportunity for learning from experience that such feelings, which we usually relegate to infants and very young children, are indeed ubiquitous, that such anxieties continue to exist to some degree in all of us throughout life. Knowing about them from within ourselves increases our perceptiveness and understanding of others. It made the group of teachers identify and sympathise with those they taught, aware in a renewed affective way of what it might be like on the first day, whether at primary or secondary school, at university or adult education centre. They began to ask themselves how little we take this into account in caring for those who stand at the beginning, where the new unknown situation tends to cause all sorts of frightening ideas to float up from the depths of the mind.

We also know in theory that we cannot pay attention to what is said when our minds are preoccupied. All the same it came as a shock to realise that well over a half of my short introductory remarks had not been heard at all, so dominant had been the affective experience of being a newcomer on a course, in a new group, in a strange institution, and the need to find means of combating the anxieties aroused. What had been heard had mostly been misunderstood and only a negligible amount of what had correctly been taken in was subsequently retained. It made us aware how a child finding himself in a large classroom might at first be too bewildered to pay any attention to the lesson. It made one wonder about the meaningfulness of assemblies at the beginning of a school year and large gatherings of college entrants. Whatever other useful functions they may serve, such as demonstrating corporateness or the authority of the staff group, as a means of imparting anything but the most elementary information, they seem at best a waste of time – at worst to heighten confusion and anxiety. When our mind is filled with anxiety, we need to find an outlet for our feelings, to express them in words or actions, find some comfort. If we are given none of these chances we tend to withdraw into ourselves or find other ways of escaping from the overwhelming experience. It was observed by a very perceptive teacher that some people had folded their arms as if to hold onto themselves and erect a barrier between themselves and their neighbour. Another teacher said that he'd found himself touching his mouth, then lit a cigarette to control his anxiety and comfort himself. Note that there were both physical and mental components active in this new situation – a feeling of coldness, of trembling, of wanting something in the mouth like a baby clinging to the breast, an arm around to comfort oneself and keep out something dangerous. These matters are very rarely talked about because we regard them as totally out of keeping with our perception of ourselves as adults, we tend to ignore such observations because we find it shameful and embarrassing to face them in ourselves and others.

Even quite young children tend to be ashamed of revealing how frightened they are in a new situation, and mobilise their most grown-up capacity to help them: 'I have a train at home just like that one,' said 3-year-old Tony, holding tightly onto the one familiar object in the unfamiliar surroundings of his new nursery. By finding something known he could, to some extent, deny the difference between nursery and home, between here and there. On his first day at school, 5-year-old Peter announced, 'I am a big brave boy now, my little brother is just a silly baby, he cries when mummy leaves him.' Being afraid to be lost, abandoned, confused is felt to be 'just a silly baby', something to be despised, and out of harmony with the school child's view of himself as grown-up and independent. Yet given the chance to speak about such feelings by an understanding teacher, children will confide. I was told by a headmaster that he regularly puts aside some time during the first two weeks of the academic year for his 11-year-old new boys to talk about their feelings. It was astounding to him to discover how free they felt once they were encouraged to do so, to talk to him. Most of them said they would never tell mummy and daddy, some tell granny or grandad how they are feeling about coming to school, and hardly any of them dared to tell their older brothers or sisters for fear of being laughed at. Mostly they chose pets; as one boy put it, 'I whispered it all into my cat's ears.' And what is the kind of thing that you can only confide to pets? Matters like: 'I was terrified of the teacher and the headmaster especially. I thought I might be examined, cut open like in an operation and that all the mess inside will show.' 'I was frightened of the other boys, I thought they'd be bullies.' 'I couldn't sleep last night, in my dream there was a whole crowd shooting at me.' 'I thought I'd be failed, not found to be good enough for this school.' As adults we consider that we have, or should have, totally outgrown such baby feelings, and that if we have not there must be something wrong with us.

The roots in infancy

It is of course true that these feelings are child-like, but we tend to treat them in a derogatory way as childish or babyish. By child-like I mean that such anxieties have their roots in our childhood and infancy. What the psycho-analytic study of the mind has shown is that experiences right from the beginning of life, and in fact the earlier back they go the more powerful their influence, remain with us in the depths of the mind throughout our lives, and are re-evoked in any situation that in any way resembles the past. This is often not in any conscious sense of remembering what it felt like; it is rather that there is a memory in feeling (as Melanie Klein called it), in our bodily and emotional states or phantasies. Thus any new situation re-awakes the feelings of being pushed out at birth from a familiar environment into one that is cold, strange and terrifying. The event of birth is perhaps the greatest change that we ever have to face, a change from a fluid environment where we are automatically fed and held within the warmth of the womb, to being outside in cold aerial boundariless surroundings where the newborn has to take over some of the physical functions. Unlike other creatures, human beings are born extremely helpless. It is this helplessness which intensifies extreme fear, nay terror. It will be helpful if this transition is made less terrifying by a warm, holding environment. The French doctor, Leboyer, has demonstrated how this dramatic experience can be made less traumatic by trying to, at first, re-create as much of the internal situation as possible. This includes providing warm physical contact by putting the baby on the mother's stomach before the cord is cut, allowing the baby to be fed as soon as possible, and immersing the newborn in a bath while gently massaging him. It is fascinating to watch on film how this reduces the fearful cry of the newborn and enables him to gradually relax and explore the world around him. It is helpful if the mother goes on introducing the world into the baby's life 'in small doses', as Dr Winnicott put it. While good experiences lay the foundation to hope that we will be helped in the process of facing painful transitions, extreme anxiety states do remain as memory traces within all of us. For any new situation involves loss of the old, known one. They are particularly likely to be re-awakened by sudden or extreme changes. The more unstructured and strange a new situation, the further we are removed from what is familiar physically, mentally or emotionally, the more disorientated and terrified we tend to feel.

But surely, you will say, unlike the baby the adult and even the child has knowledge and ability to put against his fears of being helpless, lost and confused. When he is frightened he can move away from danger, he has physical strength to defend himself, he can ask for directions, find his way back to some helpful person. And of course only in extreme situations of stress do most of us experience anything approaching the extremes or the panic of infancy. How well someone can deal with a new situation will depend on a store of good experiences in his mind; in as far as he has come to trust mother and father, and is able to hold on to such good helpful figures in their absence, he can tolerate being left on his own. On the basis of good internalised experiences we can dare to extend ourselves physically, mentally and emotionally, to venture forward and explore new people, new places, new situations – the unknown. It is true also that every added skill and every successfully negotiated task gives us some confidence in meeting a new situation. Thus a child of three is usually more dependent on the service of his parents and hence bound to feel correspondingly more afraid when he finds himself on his own, than a 16-year-old or an adult student.

But however mature and capable we are, we continue to harbour some dread of helplessness, of being lost, overcome with fear of disintegration. Even if we have mastered other like situations, we dread that our abilities will not be adequate *this* time or to *this* situation. It would seem that at every turning point we feel threatened with not knowing *where we are*, *what we are*, *who we are*. We need to test, and fear to test, whether our painfully acquired internal equipment, which is the basis of our sense of self, will stand up to the new experience or alternatively whether the boundary of the self will disintegrate under the impact of the strange situation. For we have come to know ourselves not in isolation, but in relation to others, to the known faces and surroundings; in the first instance in relation to a mother who knew and understood us. We are afraid that we may lose knowing ourselves, our identity, when all familiarity has gone and we dare to risk being face to face with the unknown. The more unfamiliar and unstructured the situation we find ourselves in, the further we are removed from home-ground physically, mentally or emotionally, the more terrified and disorientated we tend to feel. We are afraid that, like once long ago, we might again be overwhelmed by experiencing helplessness, chaos, panic at being pro-jected into a strange, separate existence.

Thus student teachers also are extremely vulnerable to being frightened of being in charge of a class. They, like a new mother or father, need support of one another and elders to face this situation. In addition to taking on a very responsible task, their own infantile anxieties are re-awakened by the children they care for. Whenever we are required to perform a new task, we may fear that, whatever we have achieved in the past, our internal store of knowledge and skills might have got lost meanwhile. We cannot even ever be sure of being able to produce a similar piece of work again whether this be an essay, a speech, a lecture, or a work of art. A teacher, in facing his new class, is also having an experience of newness and may dread whether he will be up to what this new situation will require of him. While this may be particularly true of a new group that he has to deal with, if he is at all aware of the new challenges, he will go on finding each day a new experience to some extent, and hence each time there will be some anxiety about how he will stand up to the new task. These feelings cannot be avoided, they are an inevitable concomitant of any true beginning. Indeed the negative capability of being in a state of not knowing is a prerequisite for learning and discovery. For if we are too frightened to allow ourselves to be open enough to have an emotional experience of newness we also shut ourselves off from the perception of something different, from discovering anything new, producing anything fresh. If, however, we do not thus rigidify our thinking and affects, we pay the price of the agony of helplessness, confusion, dread of the unknown – of being in a state of beginning once more.

Different kinds of hopes and fears

If we look back on the comments made by the teachers, they seem to me to fall into three categories:
(a) feeling lost and confused;
(b) hopes and fears in relation to myself, the person in authority;
(c) hopes and fears in relation to other members of the group.
I would like to examine each of these in turn and go on to consider how, in the light of these feelings, we manage the psycho-social transitions in educational establishments.

Anxieties about feeling lost

'I didn't know where to go, even when the receptionist told me, I opened the wrong doors.'

'This is such a big building with so many corridors leading off – like a maze.'

'I felt lost and confused.'

'I wanted to draw close to my neighbour in order to feel less cut off.'

'I feel a sense of isolation and am glad that the chairs were nearly touching and the room so small.'

These comments made us aware of the partial disorientation all of us experience in new surroundings. There seemed to be a wish to draw close boundaries so as to feel less exposed to a limitless void and begin to sort out in spatial terms the areas of known, as opposed to the unknown territory. It reminds us of the baby's need to be enveloped by mother's arms in order to feel held in place and protected against the strange, feared outside world. We tend to ignore that the environment must provide some corresponding holding situation for older children and adults alike if they are to feel safe. This need for boundaries is generally recognised by teachers of nursery classes in infant schools. It has become fairly common practice to keep the little ones separate, to have a special entrance and a special playground well-fenced off from the rest of the school. It would be useful if these provisions could be extended to reception classes of 5-year-olds. The separated area serves the purpose of protecting the little ones physically from the rougher older children – a kind of safe harbour. In addition, it may also be seen as providing a limited area for exploration, where they can feel held and enclosed, physically close to one another, and near to the protective adults. In this way, it is an extension of the child's experience of home, of being within a protective shell, of going so far afield without getting lost, within reach of his base, sheltered against the limitless frightening expanse. This desire for closeness was expressed by the teacher who was glad the room was small and the chairs nearly touching, as this counteracted to some extent the experience of isolation and lostness.

As well as being assured by a well-defined spatial boundary, there is the security which derives from being held within the span of some reliable person's watchful eyes. It means some safeguard against harm, just like, for instance, my entrance was experienced by some of the teachers as protecting them against the group's potential violence. To be held in someone's attention, once mother's, now the teacher's or other adult-in-charge provides us not only with some feeling of being safely watched, but at a deeper level it also means to be thought about, known as a person. In this way, we feel reassured that we exist as a separate, knowable entity. The remark made by the teacher who was anxious to establish whether a chair had been left for her, seemed to me to express concern as to whether she had been remembered. 'If no-one knows where I am, my mummy may not find me, and I might forget my name and where I live,' said a very worried 4-year-old, poignantly verbalising the fear that unless someone holds us in their mind, knows where we are, who we are, we might be utterly lost. We might ourselves forget our name, our identity, where we belong – and that indeed is terrifying. One 5-year-old would not stay at school unless mother took his coat home with her. I suspect that this signified that he wanted to leave a part of himself with mother so that she was bound to remember that she had a little boy who fitted inside this coat and would come to collect him. Other children refuse at first to take their coats off, wanting to keep within a protective skin, which acts as a kind of space suit against feeling so exposed 'in the air'. Yet others need to keep an item of mother's belongings, 'a bit of mummy' to hold on to. At one infant school, name labels were pinned on to each child's jacket. Little Amanda was seen to cling tightly to hers and anxiously reminded her mother each morning that she must not forget to put it on. A few days later she announced that she no longer needed it, 'the teacher knows my name now,' she said happily. Her relief and her greater ease at parting from mother made it clear that now she was 'known', remembered as a person by the teacher, held in her mind and therefore it was no longer necessary for her to hold on so desperately to her 'identity kit'.

While young children are particularly beset by such anxieties they apply to quite a degree to boys and girls moving from primary to junior school. Not only do the buildings become bigger and therefore more confusing, but so do the numbers of strangers to be dealt with. Some teachers visit the youngsters in their old school before the move. Even if the teacher cannot remember each child and its previous setting, the child will feel that there is a familiar person, a link with his past. Some enlightened junior schools allow new entrants to come for an orientation-day, and make sure that the pupils stay in the classroom with the same teacher for the first few days. Similar consideration might well be given to children moving up to secondary schools where they find themselves not only amongst vast numbers of others, but also with boys and girls twice their size. When students come to university it is usually taken too readily for granted that they are longing to get away from adults. We tend to forget how lonely most youngsters feel so far from home for the first time. While they may not wish to be closely supervised, they need to feel that there are adults readily available to turn to in case of need and that someone cares about them. A Freshers' cocktail party does little more than make most young people feel socially inept, unable to be jolly and superficially at ease. Some universities appoint older students to act as guides who help the newcomers to orientate themselves and settle in. Staff tutors vary greatly in their capacity to create the kind of relationship with students which expresses care and concern for them as individuals. It would seem essential that students should have ready access to their tutors so that they can discuss any problems as they arise rather than having to wait for a major crisis to erupt.

Hopes and fears in relation to teacher and institution

Thus far we have concentrated on feelings associated with a new situation and the need to find someone who cares, to whom we matter, who modulates the impact of the strange new experience. Let us now take a closer look at the kind of attitudes my teacher-group expressed in relation to me on our first evening together.

My entrance had been anxiously anticipated so that I should 'take control' – apparently to relieve the fear that something frightening, perhaps violent, would happen in the absence of a leader. Thus I seemed to be imbued with strength and power to keep violence, but also confusion and uncertainty in check. The teacher who wondered whether I had arranged the chairs so that people would feel comforted by physical closeness had an image of me as a helpful, benign person, someone who understood what it was like to feel isolated and lost and took steps to minimise the stress. A considerable amount of trust must have been invested in me to enable feelings, particularly negative ones, to be expressed so frankly. On the other hand the lady who feared there might be no chair for her must have had some concept of an uncaring organiser to whom she as an individual did not matter. Those who feared that I would be angry at their lateness or dared not speak for fear of saying something 'wrong' clearly had some picture of me as a critical, disapproving, intolerant, even perhaps potentially punitive person. The most negative view was held by the teacher who thought that members were being secretly watched, and that the rules and controls were all the more threatening because they were not spelt out. Some Kafkaesque, undefined, hidden, extremely malevolent authority had been attributed to me and/or the institution of which I was a part.

Any new relationship tends to arouse hope and dread, and these exist side by side in our minds. The less we know about the new person the freer we are to invest him with extremes of good and bad qualities. Thus these phenomena may be especially prevalent at the beginning before we have had a chance to check our conjectures, our inner hopes and fears against reality. Just as new situations re-awaken feelings of earlier days, so meeting someone new, particularly someone on whom we are to some extent dependent, whether teacher, counsellor, doctor, nurse or employer, evokes childhood wishes and anxieties. These helpers are often imbued with immense power for good and evil. They are expected to lead us into the land of happiness (like fairy godmothers), instantly quench thirst for knowledge, transmit skills, cure and take away our troubles with a wave of the wand, thus avoiding the frustration and pain of slowly gained relief, improvement, learning and growth. Alternatively, they are felt to withhold their magic, wisdom, comfort, out of spite; to attack and humiliate us with biting, destructive remarks and actions, relegate us to suffering and waiting and persecute us like demons; to punish us for our shortcomings like revengeful all-seeing gods, or tantalise us with promises only to thwart us. In however sophisticated form, such child-like notions are present in all of us to some extent. They may appear, for instance, as a demand that the lecturer should impart an easily inimitable technique of counselling and if he does not do this, he may be felt to meanly keep these skills to himself in order to be superior and let the students remain in a state of ignorance and impotence. Alongside such wonderful and terrible expectations, there are usually more realistic ones which hence may be fulfilled. These may include a desire to be helped by someone who has more knowledge and experience, the hope that one's struggles will be treated with tolerance, and one's unreasonable demands and behaviour be understood yet met with firmness.

Hopes and fears in relation to the peer-group

Because they find themselves in an analogous situation, members of one's peer-group may be expected to undergo similar emotional distress and might be turned to for support. 'I am looking to see if I know anyone,' and 'I want to be close to someone,' as well as the ensueing lively conversation at coffee break, suggested that members of the group sought some comfort from each other. Like brothers and sisters one's peers may be felt to be closer to one's experience and hence more easily confided in than the parents or teachers. They also might be sought out as potential allies against the adults in authority. Yet to establish closeness, one must be confident of a sympathetic reaction, dare to test out whether the other feels likewise, or at least understand one's reactions. Past experience of helpful friends or siblings encourages an approach to other members in the group. But there are also factors which operate against such trust. Like older brothers or sisters, fellow students might be thought to feel far more secure and grown-up than oneself. Worse still, they may, like Peter, regard one as a 'silly baby' for harbouring such anxieties. They are also rivals and thus might be out to get more attention, praise, approval from parents or teachers by doing and saying 'the right thing'. They are therefore suspected of wishing to show their superiority by criticising, humiliating, ridiculing, and treating one's efforts with contempt. Hence while looking for friends, we are wary in case they may turn out to be foes.

'Why have I been chosen?' suggests that there is also a mental relationship to those other potential students who have not been admitted. They are felt to be like unborn brothers and sisters, not given the chance of life. The remark also implies some obligation to justify one's existence on the course, or in a particularly good school, and having to deserve the privilege of having been offered a place by doing well. It seemed to carry some feeling of guilt at having got there while others have been excluded, and doubts about the capacity to fulfil the trust and hope put into one by those who made the selection. If, of course, the school or university is felt to be second or third-rate, the situation is very different.

The peers may then be felt to be rejects, and hated for being inferior like oneself. The anger might be turned against fellow students, or alternatively utilised to gang up with them against the institution.

External and internal factors which heighten stress

The foundation of our future relationship with the children and students in our educational institutions are laid right at the start. It behoves us, therefore, to carefully consider how we help or hinder these important psycho-social transitions. We have seen that anxieties on entering a new situation are inevitable and indeed necessary to emotional and intellectual growth. However, while anxiety, if not excessive, is a spur to development, exposure to too much stress or a particular individual's intolerance to such stress may either lead him to be totally unable to cope with the new situation, or drive him to adopt defensive measures that do not allow him to make full use of his potential. The way and extent to which anyone is affected by a beginning depends on the balance between the degree and nature of the external pressure and the inner resources to deal with them. There will always be some individuals so vulnerable that any change may result in disintegration, or at least a serious set-back. On the other hand, the institutional organisation might be one that makes it unduly difficult for any new-comers to adjust. In most cases, we are dealing with the combination of these factors, i.e. of unfavourable external circumstances exacerbating the individual's personal difficulties.

Those at risk on the point of transition

In each new situation we recapitulate some of the earlier anxiety situations. Our ability to encounter and make use of a new phase depends on our inner stability, the extent to which we have been able to develop an inner sense of security in the absence of the known external situation or person. Here are some of the factors which make new beginnings particularly stressful for some individuals:

(i) those who have had frequent changes of mothering and/or fathering in infancy and early childhood, each change undermining the trust in the reliability of a helping adult;

(ii) those who have experienced traumatic separations through illness and death of a parent in early childhood – such events undermine the trust in the strength and survival of the loved person in one's absence;

(iii) individuals who have not been able to internalise a good enough

experience because:
  (a) their mothers were unable to provide a sufficiently safe hold-
       ing situation,
       or
  (b) the child is so intolerant of *any* frustration that any withdrawal
       of the mother results in the destruction of the memory of the
       good experience.
  In both cases, no safe internal equipment can be acquired. These
  children and adults therefore tend to cling to an external static situation for to them any change spells disaster;
  (iv) those who have recently experienced loss or separation and may
       therefore already be psychically overloaded at this particular
       moment of time.

Factors in present relating to degree of stress

Space: the bigger the unknown space in which we find ourselves, the more
we tend to feel lost. While we may not be able to help the size of the
buildings, or the campus, it is possible to provide some security by giving
clear directions and to arrange for new entrants to be moved around as
little as possible. This is contrary to the common practice in many senior
schools, where teachers stay put, but pupils have to take themselves and
their belongings after every lesson to another classroom. This is particularly unsettling and confusing for beginners. It does not allow pupils to
feel 'at home' in any one area and leads to carelessness in relation to
property. The relation of the different parts of a school or campus to one
another are also important factors in increasing or minimising the feelings
of being in a maze, an uncohesive, uncontaining institution. Attention
needs to be given to the provision of functional areas which act as a
natural social focal point like games rooms in secondary schools and
kitchens in student colleges.

Numbers: similar considerations apply to numbers as to space: the
greater the number, the more frightening the situation becomes. We need
to get to know people in small doses. We can deal more comfortably with
meeting one or two people at first who stay to act as guides and introduce
us to a small group and later a widening circle. We feel most lost in a large
group, afraid of hostility and violence and loss of our identity. Furthermore a high degree of subject choice may mean that the membership of
one's peer group is constantly changing. This is extremely unsettling for it
provides no opportunity to establish cohesive relationships. On the other
hand, teaching in individual tutorials if not supplemented by small
seminar groups may lead to too much isolation and lack of opportunity to
find congenial companions.

↑

Strangeness: it is self-evident that the more removed the new situation is from previous ones, the more bewildering and frightening it is likely to be. A child or adult from a home-background or culture vastly different from that of the school or college has thus the additional problem of facing unfamiliar ways of thinking, relating, behaving – even the signs whereby he judges whether he fits in or not may be difficult for him to fathom. The disorientation and confusion will be correspondingly great. We would therefore need to give special help to those new-comers.

Interaction of external and internal factors: brief case illustrations

Beginning school

Jane had been eagerly waiting to be old enough to go to school like her brothers and sisters. When the big day arrived, she stalked away proudly, with hardly a backward glance at her mother. It came as a great surprise to her mother, therefore, when she complained on the following day that other children were 'horrid', school 'boring' and told her of the 'lunch lady' insisting that she clear her plate. After the first week-end she was tearful, had a stomach ache and begged to stay at home.

While enthusiasm and eagerness may be appropriate, one should always be a little suspicious of a child who shows no sign of worry at parting from mother and beginning a very new experience. Subsequent talks with Jane revealed that she had held a too rosy, too idealised picture of school-life. Her complaint that it was boring covered her disappointment that she had not been instantly enabled to read and write and become like her much admired brothers and sisters. Behind her confident air had lain an expectation that relationships at school would be just like those at home where as the youngest she had received special attention from her parents and been treated with benign tolerance by the older children. She was therefore surprised and frightened by her school mates' assertiveness and unable to fight back, and disappointed at being just one of the crowd.

There are multiple factors which led to Jane's school refusal which might in time have built up into a full-blown school phobia. I have outlined how her home situation played into her unrealistic expectations of school and made the beginning so particularly disappointing and traumatic. No doubt her parents' high intellectual standards were also partly to blame for Jane's ambitions. But let us look at what the school might have contributed. Jane had visited the classroom with her mother in the summer term, as is the usual practice with potential pupils. She had thus seen children actually able to read and write. There was evidence of their achievements spread all round the walls! How was she to know that it had taken her predecessors quite a few months to learn to accomplish this? The impressions gained might indeed have been misleading, prompted less by the school's concern to cater to the new entrant's needs than by the wish to impress the parents. Too much emphasis is still put on intellectual attainments and competition is often encouraged at the expense of good social relationships. Teachers tend to devalue the role they play in helping children become members of a group. They are usually unaware that they are responsible for handling one of the most delicate moments in a child's life. It would help them in this task if they were to engage in detailed discussions with the parents before the child begins at school. They might thus enquire about the child's concept of school, the nature of his relationship with adults of different sexes and children of the same and different age-groups. Well-briefed, the teacher may then be more sensitive to the special strengths and weaknesses of each child, able to help him both in class and in the playground.

Jane was fortunate in that her mother and teacher got together before the situation grew worse. Mother was allowed to stay for a few days at the back of the classroom. Once she left, the teacher kept Jane close to her for a little while and ensured that she was well supervised in her play with others. Jane was also permitted to bring a packed lunch and was thus able to feel that she could take a bit of home with her to school. Food is so deeply embedded in the child's whole relationship with mother that school meals need to be given far more thought and attention. They are often a focus for the child's complaints about the school. As in Jane's case, it may be necessary, at least for a while, to allow a child to keep a concrete proof of his relationship to the mother by bringing her food to school.

In many schools, food is served by special 'lunch ladies'. Sometimes these impose rigid standards which means that eating can become a routine, divorced from relating to children as individuals. Most lunch ladies are kind and homely older women who perform a very important mothering function for the children. They and janitors and other non-teaching staff are sometimes the most loved and trusted of the school personnel and the ones that children will turn to for comfort or in whom they confide their worries. It is regrettable that their contribution is so seldom recognised by the teaching staff or their knowledge of individual children drawn upon.

Difficulties arising from joining late

Paul was referred to the psychologist some six months after entering secondary school. He was known to be a bright boy but had rapidly fallen far behind the rest of the form. He had not acquired any friends, appeared shy and inattentive. In his conversations with the psychologist, it became clear that Paul was so pre-occupied with feeling lost, bewildered and frightened, that he was quite unable to concentrate on school work. He had been sick when term started and so had had to join the school a month later than all the other children. He felt that while they all knew where to put their clothes, their sports-gear, where the different classrooms were situated, how to get permission for working in the library, he had no idea how to go about these things. He did not want to ask for fear of appearing stupid. So he found himself constantly trailing behind others, afraid of making false moves. He had come from a small school where he was amongst the best, to a very big one where he felt lost, silly and uncared for. He also voiced his fear that in this large school the teachers could not possibly keep an eye on all the boys and therefore did not know what secret and violent things went on. One of the big boys in a higher form had offered Paul drugs, and when he refused had threatened that the gang would be after him if he told the teachers. So he had kept quiet and felt burdened by this guilty secret and yet afraid of being set upon by older boys.

This example makes us aware of two things: (1) the need to help a late-comer to settle in, for in addition to the usual problem of being new, Paul felt himself to be the odd one out, the *only* one who did not know the way to behave and act; (2) the need for teachers to be far more vigilant at what happens out of the classroom, in school corridors, changing rooms, on the way out of school. Of course it is not possible nor desirable to constantly supervise growing children but it is important to be aware of tensions, of trouble-makers and intimidators, and thus able to protect children from frightening, unhappy situations which are beyond their capacity to deal with unaided. Consultation between psychologist and school staff led to Paul being allowed to work for a period of time in the library. The more sheltered situation and the relationship to a trusted adult enabled him to contain his anxieties and under these conditions it did not take long before he caught up with his studies and became generally a more integrated member of the school.

Difficulties of a first-year university student

Gerald had got into a dangerous cycle of drinking and drug-taking within the first few weeks of coming to university. He had also taken a mild over-dose. When he was interviewed, he said that he felt lonely and depressed, unwanted and uncared for. It became apparent that leaving home and coming to university had revived earlier, more infantile anxieties about being left when mother had given birth to a succession of younger sisters and brothers. Each time he had felt ousted and leaving home seemed to be experienced at depth as the final expulsion from his mother's care.

Although this young man clearly brought to the situation a particular personal vulnerability of feeling rejected and abandoned it was evident that the provisions made for him did nothing to help him overcome depression and loneliness. Living in digs in town removed him from the centre of activities on the campus and of natural opportunities to mix with others. The campus itself appeared to him vast, underlining his feeling lost in an impersonal world. Nor did he feel contained in a defined structure of relationships. As he said: 'one is a nobody, travelling around in a vast space, in an endlessly changing succession of groups to which one doesn't belong. No one cares whether you are alive or dead. They wouldn't even know about it. I was aware that I could have contacted my tutor, but he has not given any indication of being particularly interested in me and I didn't think I could go and tell him that I am just plain unhappy.'

The care of the doctor and student counsellor subsequently enabled this young man to feel that he could turn to them for help, instead of having to resort to drowning his sorrows in drink and kill off his despair with sleeping pills. He also decided that he would feel less lonely if he moved into a hall of residence where he could turn to other students and feel part of a peer group. There are students who, unlike Gerald, join delinquent groups simply in order to have a sense of belonging. It would seem important that we provide conditions of personal care by staff and mature students so as to allow new-comers to gradually come to find valuable new human relationships of a constructive kind. Otherwise they might fall back on the wrong kind of friends, or the wrong kind of defensive behaviour, getting rid of painful feelings by drugging them, drowning them or behaving violently. We want, after all, not to provide blind alleys but openings to further development.

Part II

Learning to understand the nature of relationships
I.Salzberger-Wittenberg

Chapter 2

Aspects of the student's relationship to the teacher

Introduction

Beginnings are beset, as we have seen, by many fears and hopes. At that point we are still mainly dealing with preconceptions and expectations based on the past. The actual nature of the relationship has yet to be tried out and learnt from. So let us see what happens subsequent to the first encounter with reality.

The first meeting with the class is over. One breathes a sigh of relief that one's worst fears have not materialised. We have survived the transition, mastered the beginning somehow. If the first day has passed without too many mishaps, this is a relief and reassurance to both students and teachers alike. For those in charge, it is like having given birth to a new venture and produced a healthy baby. So much worry, preparation and anticipation is centred upon starting, that the arrival of an actual alive class or group, as indeed the arrival of a new baby, is a relief and joy in itself. We would like to lean back, rest from our labour, feel proud and be congratulated on our product. We may feel buoyed up by our achievement and in an optimistic mood, as if, having got over the worst, things will be easier from now on. But the baby, the schoolchildren, the course members do not remain still: they need to be nourished; they make demands on us; they cry out and complain when frustrated or in some mental pain. It dawns on us that the work has only just begun, that our ability to provide the right environment and mental food for students is yet to be tested. Compared to the tasks ahead, the labour pangs of giving birth to a new venture seem in retrospect, if severe, at least quickly over. We wonder what process we have set in motion, what we have taken on and whether we will be able to sustain the effort over time.

Let me return to my experience with the teachers' course. The members of the group often arrive for their second meeting apparently less anxious than to the first one. On the one hand our previous meeting

23

seems to have allayed some fears and stimulated eagerness at what is to come. On the other hand I find myself far more challenged in a direct way. Having suggested that we look at the kind of feelings that students have in relation to their teacher, and that we might use the present situation for that purpose, Mrs A says angrily, 'I don't really think there's much comparison between this class and the ones I usually find myself in as a teacher. We have to teach certain subjects, get through a curriculum. Also we have come here because we chose to, while our pupils have to attend school, so how can we learn from this course?'

I agree that in a number of ways this situation is different, but I am at once interrupted by Mr B who states firmly, ' "Situation" is an expression that's "out" these days; I, as a teacher of English, must point this out to you.' Mr C now says, 'I'm not sure I shall stay this course – I think this discussion is boring. All that I've heard so far is perfectly familiar to me.' It seems to me that such criticisms and doubts may be very relevant aspects of the reactions to a new teacher – challenging his knowledge and authority. I ask whether what they have just observed is fundamentally different from the way their students behave and feel towards them. This leads to the following contributions from members: pupils tend to argue, disagree; they often want to show that they know more than their teacher, are cleverer; that they are bored with the subject and it's not worthwhile to make an effort. These remarks seem perfectly to fit what we have just experienced, and it seems useful therefore to consider whether the kind of feelings aroused may have a bearing on understanding the student-teacher relationship. Another member of the group suggests that the group may be·afraid the new teacher is not strong enough to control them and that to challenge him is a way of testing his strength. Others suggest that while there may be such a hope, pupils tend to want to find out the teacher's weak spots in order to feel superior. They may make the teacher feel worthless or shut out, especially if a whole group gang up against him. Others mention that students easily feel belittled, judged, afraid of being found to be inferior and worthless. We seem, at this point, to move from the more hostile feelings to consider the student's wish to be liked, fed, helped, approved of, comforted, be noticed. A primary school teacher points out how much children turn to her as a kind of parent-figure, someone who will take čare of their physical as well as emotional needs. Another teacher tells us that she is used as confidante, asked to listen to the problems that a child has at home, or an adolescent with her boyfriend. Many teachers feel that a great deal of trust is put upon them by the children. They mention that there is usually a great deal of curiosity about their personal lives and there now ensues a discussion about the extent to which it is helpful to share personal information about oneself with the children. One teacher says, 'I don't want to tell them too much, I think they already envy my better economic position and my greater knowledge.' Another teacher talks about the children's phantasy about the teacher's private life and the reason for a teacher's absence. It has become clear that teachers hold an extremely important position in the mental life of their students and that they are invested very often with very strong positive and negative feelings. In examining some of the common attitudes towards teachers I would like to distinguish those which are more realistic and likely to promote a working relationship from those which, however strongly held, might be said to be anti-work, anti-learning and anti-development.

The student's expectations of the teacher

The teacher as the source of knowledge and wisdom

It is realistic to expect a teacher to have more knowledge about the subject he is offering to teach than those coming to learn from him. It is, for instance, reasonable to expect the Tavistock staff to be able to share some of the insights gained on the basis of their experience in the psycho-analytic study of human relationships and have some notions about their relevance to the field of education. However, I often find that course members hope that we would provide specialised knowledge in any number of areas well beyond the scope of our institution, such as social action and sociology. Such hopes on the part of members derive from the desire for an all-knowing teacher and preferably one who could impart omniscience to his students. Equally, many children come to school with a notion that the teacher ought to have an encyclopaedic mind which pours out facts and information, rather than someone who is concerned to help children to learn and acquire ways of finding out about the world. The wish for an all-knowing teacher stems from the childhood feelings that the parents are the possessors of all knowledge and wisdom. The insistence on the imparting of information as the primary or (even) exclusive object of education rests on the assumption that the adult knows all there is to be known and that this concrete bundle of knowledge can be taken over by the student as a package. Such a belief leads to the demand that the adult hand 'it' over; 'it' being a body of knowledge, an 'answer', a skill, a 'cure', or perfect understanding. If he does not do so, he may be experienced as withholding his riches out of meanness and spite. An example of this from the teacher's group is the frequently voiced complaint that I am not imparting a 'technique' of interviewing. The notion seems to be that the teacher's function is to provide concrete answers or demonstrate skills to be copied, rather than at best stimulating curiosity, making the student more aware of questions to be asked and helping the student to observe the phenomena that are available to his senses, and assisting him to sort such impressions against some framework of understanding. Yet I have often found that students feel angry and cheated as if one was withholding something they feel entitled to and could possess if only the teacher would be more willing to share. We detect here the kind of suspicions that some children and adolescents harbour in relation to their parents, believing that the latter are deliberately and meanly not handing over to them their grown-up capacities because they wish to exclude and deprive adolescents and keep them relegated to a state of ignorance and impotence.

Sooner or later, as the child grows up, he is bound to discover that even his powerful parents who seem to have an answer to so many of his questions, have in fact only limited knowledge. The disappointment that they don't know everything and that their answers are quite inadequate to deal with his puzzlement about the world may be so great that, far from idealising them, he now becomes disparaging of them, claiming that if they are not all-knowing then they are stupid and ignorant and have nothing to offer him at all (as indeed course members did, at times, in relation to the Tavistock staff). He may turn his back on them and look for other adults in the hope that he will find the all-knowing person who will provide the answers that ought to be available. Equally adults may seek out one instructor after the other, one course after another, not simply for enrichment but in the vain search for the ideal oracle. They may be attracted by people who appear to be clever, who have easy answers readily available, bodies of knowledge neatly stored into packages of theories. In this way they try to escape the unpalatable fact that the world is complex, our understanding of it is limited, and that if we want to find out and learn we have to face being bewildered, confused, and anxious. Maybe, however, the child or adult looking for the source of wisdom comes to the conclusion that there is *no-one* who will sort it all out for him. He will then be able to discriminate between those who are indeed good teachers and make him question, observe and think, from those who are only superficially clever and provide facile solutions. While such discovery of other people's limitations may be painful, it may stimulate him to explore for himself, and he may then find some excitement and satisfaction in his quest for the truth.

The teacher as provider and comforter

It is inherent in the learning situation that we feel to some degree dependent on our mentors. We turn to them in the hope that they will increase our understanding and skills; we rely to some extent on their greater experience and hope to profit from it; we may also look to them to provide guidance and support. We need, however, to distinguish a hopeful expectation as regards their adult abilities and willingness to help, from the more infantile demand that the teacher should be an automatic provider of all the student's needs and wishes. In all of us there is a child-part longing for the lost paradise of pre-natal existence and infancy in which needs are instantly met (or so we would like to imagine). It is easy for those coming to a course to adopt a passive attitude, expecting the lecturer to feed them information and assume that all that is required is to sit comfortably, open one's ears and perhaps write down what is being said in the hope that, in this way, one will be able to take away knowledge. 'After all,' a student may claim with an air of righteousness, he has 'come to be instructed', to have knowledge instilled in him; he may even pride himself that his submissive attitude proves that he is a 'good' pupil, obedient and attentive. This passivity is based on a belief in a kind of magic way of passing stuff which we call knowledge from one person to the other. It ignores the fact that even an infant does not have food dropped into his mouth, but has to be active, to stimulate the flow of milk by his sucking, to swallow and digest what has been taken in. Later, he will begin to move towards an exploration of the substance of things by becoming curious about mother's and his own body. He will have to be actively struggling to acquire physical and mental skills. In its most extreme form passivity may amount to parasitism, where the pupil feels that simply by being present, sitting in the classroom (like being a foetus inside the mother's uterus) he partakes of knowledge, via an umbilical cord, so to speak. Such infantile wishes are probably present to some extent in everyone and explains the ease with which pupils lapse into passivity, handing over the responsibility for their progress to the teacher. Even when this is less extreme there is a desire that learning should be made easier. The teacher who does not comply with the demand for 'spoon-feeding' is readily accused of being unhelpful and making un-reasonable demands on the student.

On our course these attitudes may show themselves in a sophisticated guise, for instance, by insisting that we ought to provide straightforward lectures on psychological theory and instructions on how to counsel. It may be quite difficult for some to realise that in the field of human relationships the teacher is quite unable, even if he should wish to do so, to hand over the capacity to be in touch with emotional conflict. A body of theory can of course be taught, but it would be a purely intellectual acquisition likely to delude its possessor into believing that he knows something about the mind when all he has got is a tool for categorising people. This is a dangerous attitude and a far cry from understanding based on empathy. It is also totally useless if the task is to learn to appreciate the individuality of each person and to provide a relationship that gives students the opportunity to develop. Our course aims to increase awareness of the conflicts of human beings by becoming more observant of others and oneself. To learn to observe is as necessary in this field as in any other and is the basis of discovery. Insistence on an easy way of obtaining knowledge and experience is a very serious hindrance to real learning and development, yet we all lapse into this state readily and frequently.

Similar problems arise in regard to the teacher as a counsellor. It may be reasonable to expect a teacher to pay attention to his student's worries, to listen and be concerned about his distress, try to alleviate it in as far as it is possible to do so, find out something about the nature of the problem and if necessary refer him for help somewhere. Some pupils, however, may make unlimited demands on the teacher, invade his free time and privacy. The student may feel no compunction about his greed but, on the contrary, professes to love his teacher and claim that he has at last found in him the only person who cares and understands him.

He is unaware that by idealising the teacher he is disregarding the teacher's real need for rest and recreation and that by taking possession of him he is avoiding pangs of jealousy in relation to the teacher's family and to the other pupils with whom he has to share him. There is probably a universal craving to return to a state of babyhood, and receive the devoted and exclusive loving care of a maternal person; something that the individual has once had or, alternatively, has never experienced but always hungered for. If indeed an adolescent or adult cannot manage without such intensive whole-time care, then the help of other professionals will have to be drawn upon. It is far beyond the scope of the teacher's task. More commonly the demands arise from the wish to escape from frustration and emotional pain.

Teachers like others in helping professions, as e.g. doctors, nurses, psychiatrists, and social workers, easily become objects of infantile hopes: someone who will magically cure pain, take away frustration, helplessness, despair, and instead provide happiness and the fulfilment of all desires. We must expect that a person who holds on to the belief that such wishes should and *can* be met will easily feel disappointed, may soon turn away from us in anger, blame us for being totally unhelpful and seek out someone who appears more likely to comply with his wishes. What is so dangerous in this attitude, and our tendency to fit in with it, is that it is anti-development, for as long as there is a persistent belief that the individual does not have to struggle with some frustration and mental pain he is not likely to discover or develop any latent strengths. Most of us do not attempt to stretch our mental muscles unless we have to. We get such ready advice, we have so many friends and books at our disposal which tell us what to do! We can use this to continue to rely excessively on outside help, yet this very dependency will add to our fear of being abandoned and resentment towards the person we depend on. If we can instead turn to others for support, understanding and comfort, not in order to rely totally on them but as temporary aids to help us in our struggles, we may gradually gain confidence in being able to learn from our own experience.

The teacher as an object of admiration and envy

The teacher who is an expert in his field may be held in high esteem. Some teachers earn our admiration by their deep interest in their subject and their unselfish devotion to the pursuit of knowledge, truth and beauty. In addition, some have the capacity to impart enthusiasm about their subject to others and have a stimulating and inspiring effect on those who come into contact with them. Thus a number of qualities in those from whom we learn may evoke admiration. This can lead to a deep appreciation and the wish to strive to become as far as possible like the admired teacher, but it can also provoke idealisation and hero-worship. The teaching that is based on idealisation may evoke a lot of keenness in the student but this is often short-lived. I remember adoring a young physics teacher. During the year he taught me I shone in this subject for the first and last time in my life. If the teacher is felt to be the ultimate authority on a subject, it may be felt that he has solved all the problems and discovered all there is to know – hence he becomes deified, his ideas treated as gospel, no-one daring to question or add to them.

There is no admiration without some degree of envy. It is a question of the relative strength of these feelings. We all wish to possess beauty, intelligence, creativity. When envy is uppermost, a person attacks and tries to destroy in a variety of ways the very thing he envies. He is usually unaware that his ridicule, snide remarks, constant criticism or rubbishing of the teacher's work are prompted by envy. An envious person is likely to be good at finding out the teacher's weak points and playing on them. He may indeed succeed in undermining the teacher's confidence, make him feel depleted, be distracted or, where envy is powerfully in operation, even unable to think. Alternatively, it may be the hopefulness or enjoyment of work that is under attack. One teacher told us that the pupils in a particular form at her school had been so destructive that they nearly 'killed' in her the desire to teach. Spoiling behaviour can indeed be so powerfully effective. One way of avoiding awareness of one's envy is to try to provoke it in others. There are students who instil a sense of inferiority in their peers and teacher by their display of brilliance, or engage in name-dropping as if connectedness with the high and mighty imparted importance. Adolescents often make their elders feel as if they already have one foot in the grave and all enjoyment of life and sexuality was the property of youth. Alternatively, some individuals assume that far from struggling to learn, one can simply *be* what one desires, get into the

'Emperor's clothes', and so evade exposure to feeling naked, poor and envious. Another way of dealing with envy is the secret stealing of knowledge. It is of course desirable for the student to use materials provided to help him to accomplish some learning by himself. It is a totally different matter when someone claims to be able to do it *all* by himself or parades the snippets of knowledge he picked up from others as the products of his own discovery. This is like a child who prefers to raid the larder rather than eat at meal-times. Such behaviour avoids acknowledgment of where physical or mental food comes from and gratitude towards the provider of it.

Admiration is bound up with comparisons between the self and the other. Such comparison may lead to rivalry and can easily involve notions of superiority and inferiority. To be in a position of a learner may be felt by an envious pupil not to be an inevitable stage in development but a deliberate attempt to *make* him feel stupid and humiliated. This evokes resentment and a rejection of what is being offered; it is thus a very serious obstacle to learning. In a less extreme form it undermines the enjoyment of the process of acquiring knowledge and skill. Some pupils do not appreciate that the teacher has had to struggle to obtain knowledge and experience. Instead he is felt to have been born with the silver spoon of wisdom in his mouth and hence to have no conception of what it is like to be a child. 'It's all right for you' is a frequent dictum, indicating that the other is felt to have come easily by his achievements.

The teacher as a judge

A respected teacher is likely to be turned to for constructive criticism. This may be helping the student to achieve better results and reach the goal which he has set himself. On the other hand any criticism is easily felt to be cutting and destructive and the teacher experienced as complaining, dissatisfied, or even as a deliberate fault-finder; in an extreme form he may be thought to want to pick holes in the work of the student in order to show up his shortcomings and make him feel inadequate. While it is part of a teacher's function to assess the student's work, this lends itself to a feeling of being constantly watched and judged. There is a fear of being found wanting, not good enough and possibly barred from taking the next step forward. The pupils' rivalry with one another also prompts the idea of being assessed on a sliding scale ranging from being top to being bottom, rather than allowed to progress at their own pace and attaining a certain required standard. If the student thinks he cannot be the top one, he may give up rather than strive to do the best he is capable of. On the other hand, he may find some satisfaction in being the worst, and hence 'special'. Pupils will wonder who is teacher's favourite, who is liked and disliked. They are very conscious of whether their contribution has captured the teacher's interest or is disregarded. I have found that comments I make in order to draw attention to a phenomenon I have observed in the group are almost invariably experienced as value judgments, implying praise or blame. It follows that students are highly sensitive to any criticism which the teacher expresses and that this often is the cause of deep distress.

The teacher as an authority figure

The role of headmaster, organiser of a course, teacher, counsellor, (as those of social worker, doctor, therapist) implies a position of some authority. Part of the job involves making decisions which affect those for whom he is responsible. This may be very limited as in the case of a teacher. His management decisions are usually confined to providing a certain setting for his work, in terms of space and time, and a minimum requirement as regards the behaviour he is willing to tolerate from his students, as well as a minimum standard of work and effort. At the other end of the scale is the headmaster who is known to be responsible for the curriculum, the rules and disciplines of the establishment, the hiring and firing of the staff, and the admission and expulsion of students. Yet all those in a position of responsibility tend to be invested with far more authority than they actually possess or wish to exercise. For example, a school counsellor may wrongly be thought to decide on a child's remaining or being sent away from school. Whether we like it or not, whether we hold certain views of our position or not, we have to be aware that students are likely to attribute considerable power to us. Their hopes and fears may be quite unrealistic and extreme. They may invest us with being a benign authority, that can bring about peace, harmony, salvation, relief from suffering. On the other hand, they may be afraid that the person in a position of authority will abuse his power. He might be a tyrant who will deprive those for whom he is responsible of their freedom, not permit any opposition and treat those dependent on him as slaves to his masterly commands. He may be thought to be someone who will inflict severe punishment. This may lead to terror and submission. Alternatively, some students have a wish to be punished so as to be absolved of guilt, and some invest the teacher with ultimate power for good or ill in order to abrogate their own responsibility.

There are of course many shades of fear of a punitive authority and degrees of belief in an ideally good one. Many students and teachers that I have met confuse the exercise of authority and limit-setting with being authoritarian, though the latter implies some degree of dictatorship, a restriction of freedom in order to control and dominate others. If the student is more realistic he may hope that the person in charge has enough authority to be able to control violence, set limits to unreasonable behaviour, treat destructiveness, negligence and sloth with strength and benevolent firmness, thereby allowing the more constructive elements of the personality and that of others in the group to come to the fore. It is the wish for a kindly but firm teacher who has enough belief in the good qualities of his pupils to set high standards, yet is not so stern as to intimidate them or show no forbearance at their inevitable mistakes and human failings.

Transference

I have indicated some of the manifold feelings that can suffuse the relationship to a teacher. These may be more or less realistic or extreme in different individuals and within the same individual at different times. They may encompass all the human emotions, but we have been particularly concerned with those that are likely to arise in a learning situation. It may appear strange to us that we should be the recipients of such powerful positive and negative feelings. They may seem unwarranted by the situation, by the way we behave and what we know of ourselves. Because we do not understand why they have arisen we tend to experience their manifestation as perturbing, finding ourselves in turn flattered or hurt by them. Most of the time we tend to disregard their presence and even if we are vaguely aware of their existence we are inclined to underestimate their strength and the powerful effect they can have on the relationship between student and teacher – and hence on the capacity to learn. We have seen, for instance, that if fear and envy or both predominate they will interfere with, or even prevent, learning. While admiration, love and gratitude may encourage effort, extreme over-idealisation of the teacher can lead to the belief that no effort is required. We may consider that such strong feelings of love and hate are nothing but a hindrance to the task of learning and teaching, yet they do exist and cannot be wished away. We can only try, by our attitude and behaviour, to encourage a more realistic concept of a helping adult which the student can then put against the extreme notions that may exist in his mind. But let us first trace the source of such infantile feelings.

The concept of the transference

It was Sigmund Freud who discovered that feelings that have been experienced in the past are *transferred* into present relationships. He found that his patients re-lived in relation to him emotional experiences which they had had in their childhood. At first he was struck by the erotic attachment to him, but later he came to see that all kinds of feelings of love, hatred, jealousy, rivalry and fear were revived. The events that the patients remembered or relived were not accurate replica of what had actually happened but were highly coloured by the patients' emotions and phantasies, their fears and wishes. Equally the individual's perception of the relationship between others was strongly influenced by their feelings towards them. Thus a child's view of the parents' sexual relationship as a cruel one may arise from his angry feelings at being excluded and in his jealousy makes them fight and hurt each other. Such phantasies may exert a strong influence on his attitude towards his own and others' sexuality and interfere with his adult relationships in later life.

Such phantasies often do not appear as memories but are alive both on a conscious and unconscious level in current relationships and deeply affect them. Freud called this phenomenon of the past being constantly revived in the present the 'transference'. The tendency to repeat past patterns of relating is a universal phenomenon and recurs in any important relationship. Freud came to the conclusion that no experience is ever lost, it remains stored in the mind and ready to be re-awakened in any situation that resembles the past in some way. Thus contact with the teacher is likely to revive in the student many of the emotions that he experienced in the past in relation to his mother and father. That these included the most primitive anxiety states dating back to earliest infancy was discovered by Melanie Klein, one of the first psychoanalysts to treat young children. She found their minds to be full of phantastic images, far more terrifying and far more wonderful than any real parents. They resembled the figures found in fairy tales: witches, monsters and demons who perpetrate evil and evoke terror; fairy god-mothers, genies and magicians who fulfil every wish and bring about transformations in an instant. She hypothesised that the child had created idealised pictures of his parents in order to counteract his extreme fears of a hostile environment. These fears and fearful images are related to the state of helplessness of the baby in the face of pain and frustration, but receive added impetus from the angry destructive feelings within him. Like Freud, she believed that the human being is born with a duality of impulses, with love *and* hate, which colour his perception of the world from the beginning of life. Klein's work provides a deeper insight into the rich phantasy world of the child. Every physical experience was seen to have a mental counterpart, a 'phantasy' attached to it. On the other hand phantasies were experienced as if they were concrete happenings; thus thoughts are felt by the child to have actual effects on others in the outside world. Not only children, but adults too, to some extent, experience thoughts to be omnipotent and have consequences, fearing for instance that the murderous thoughts one harbours will cause actual harm to others.

The continuous conflict between love and hate

Mrs Klein's work confirmed Freud's finding that constructive and destructive impulses are constantly at war with one another, threatening to produce a state of tension in relation to the outside world and within the individual's mind. By keeping love and hate separate, associating and identifying with the good and idealised aspects and getting rid of and attributing bad qualities to others, the pain of inner conflict can to some extent be avoided, as can the conflict with the persons we love.Thus the clinging, controlling, demanding behaviour of a child towards his mother may be seen as an attempt to maintain his loving feelings and keep at bay the angry feelings towards her, the fear of losing her and being left in a frightened state.

As adults, we may no longer believe in fairy-tale creatures, but there remains a tendency to hope for magic, particularly in situations of stress. Hence we turn for instance to doctors with an unrealistic belief in their omnipotent power for good or evil. We may also attribute the events in our lives to some unknown source, an external force, being favoured by the gods, persecuted by an evil fate or punished for our sins. In a less extreme vein, we are inclined to see others and the events in our lives with a halo-effect of goodness or badness, benign or persecuting.

While most of us achieve a more balanced view some of the time, there are those who cling permanently to the division into wonderful and terrible, black and white. Nothing is good enough, it has to be heavenly or 'dreadful', the latter usually leading to a grievance, to a feeling of unfairness at not possessing the ideal others are believed to own. No attempt is made to look at the facts or how the dreaded or disappointing situation has come about, for the belief in some phantastic ideal somewhere is kept alive by powerful motives. Such a belief is to spare us the emotional pain which is involved in accepting reality; it is to prevent us from feeling ignorant and helpless; it is to keep us from the awareness of our destructiveness in the face of frustration and limitations; it is to save us from the painful conflict which arises when we find ourselves hating the very person we love. We can then avoid the worry that our greedy demands or behaviour may do harm, our lack of concern be a burden to others and cause them suffering. If we can departmentalise love and hate, keeping our regard and idealisation for those with whom we identify and denigrating and seeing only badness in others, e.g. the bad teacher, the despised member of a group (or certain groups in the family of nations), then we can avoid some very painful inner conflicts. But idealisation of ourselves and our group is likely to break down in the face of reality and can only be maintained at the price of increased denial and hatred of others to whom all undesired qualities are attributed. This leads to constant strife in our social relationships.

In each new encounter, hope of a perfect relationship may be revived and we are then likely to go through a stage of illusion followed by disillusionment. One of the teachers in our group commented that most of the classes she takes over are well-behaved at first, but later 'all hell breaks loose'. Some degree of anger is to be expected, for when our attempt to escape unpalatable facts (e.g. knowing so very little or finding others less than ideal) fails, we try to vent our anger and blame someone for the unsatisfactory world we live in, for having to bear frustration, doubt and fear, for the fact that we are imperfect human beings grappling with other imperfect human beings.

While phantasies influence the perception of reality to some extent, reality is constantly tested by our senses. Thus the actual provision of care given by parents and others is of immense importance in confirming or alleviating the child's fears, in strengthening or undermining his hope, or providing a realistic picture of helping parental figures. What is transferred is therefore far more than infantile hopes and fears: it is the whole picture of the world that an individual has gradually built up in his mind as a result of his interaction with others. His hope may have been strengthened, his fears alleviated by the external world. For from the very beginning of life the individual develops the structure of his personality through an intimate contact with others. Thus mother and father may have helped to foster hope and trust in reliable, caring adults; or by repeatedly not meeting his needs or by leaving him, they may have undermined his hope and instead created an expectation that adults are untrustworthy, unreliable, or non-understanding. The child's experiences may have created a picture of others strong enough to withstand his destructive acts and able to help him control them. Alternatively, if important figures in his life were easily overwhelmed or struck down by illness or death, it will have confirmed his fears of being omnipotently destructive. This makes some individuals afraid of any aggression and leads them to inhibit it or feel constantly laden by guilt while others rebel against their overstrict, overburdened conscience by taking no responsibility for their destructiveness. Adults in the child's life may have increased the fear that others are in fact violent and exploitive, or helped him to maintain some trust that they fundamentally care, in spite of his and their own shortcomings.

Transference in the learning situation

The young child who comes to school, the adult at college, has been patterned not by one sequence of inter-play between inner and outer events, but by myriads of them which will have gradually created a very individual and unique pattern of relationships in his mind. It is this internal picture of the world and the relationships between himself and others (as well as between others) which is transferred into the new situation. This internal picture leads to assumptions about the external world, which, as R. Gosling has stated, influences the present in three important ways. It affects: (a) the way we perceive, (b) the way we interpret, (c) the way we behave. An example of (a) is of a boy who adores his mother and has been the apple of her eye. He may expect to seduce his teacher (as he did his mother) by his charm rather than feel a need to earn praise by hard work and achievement. An example of (b) is of a girl who has an ailing father and who interprets her teacher's absence invariably as a sign that she has been too much of a burden to him. An example of (c) is a young man who, expecting punishment, behaves so outrageously that he eventually drives his teacher to act in a punitive manner.

These examples show that we do not need to unravel a person's past history in order to understand him. If we are observant, we can gain insight into his assumptions and beliefs from his behaviour and reactions to ourselves and others in the here and now. Awareness of the transference elements enables us to have some space to think about the nature of the relationship, to take a more objective view of it. Thus we may be able to resist being carried away by the flattering adulation of an adolescent, recognising instead that we are merely at the moment the embodiment of a longed-for dream-figure and are being seen through rose-tinted spectacles in order to maintain a desired illusion. It may also make us modestly aware that the love and trust with which a child comes to school is likely to be in a large measure due to his own loving impulses, strengthened by good relations at home, rather than attributable to ourselves.

By the same token, the suspiciousness and hostility of a student may be less readily felt as a personal attack which wounds us or makes us angry. The teacher may be better able to distinguish between a student trusting him enough to bring his negative feelings to him, and the one who has a real negative transference in terms of his envy of the teacher's good qualities or his mistrust of him as a caring person. All these attitudes might be examined to see how much they are part of the student's deeply held convictions carried forward into the new situation. We need, however, to consider carefully what factors in the present situation, such as our behaviour, may be provoking or fitting in with the student's unrealistic fears and hopes. For while it is important to be aware of the influence of the past, this should not be taken to mean that everything is attributable to it. Whatever individuals bring to a new situation, they have some awareness of reality and continually compare their actual experience with preconceived ideas (unless they are so extremely disturbed as to be not in touch with outer reality). If the teacher can provide a different experience from the one that is feared or unrealistically desired, the pupil has another chance to adjust his picture of the world and grow on the basis of this new experience. We are however likely to be type-cast in accordance with his assumptions and be propelled to enact the script of his internal play. Hence it is difficult and yet of the greatest importance not to behave like puppets on a string, yielding to the pressure to conform to the students' expectations in as far as these are unrealistic. The teacher, for instance, who is aware of being idealised but resists rising to the bait, is helping the student by his example to continue to strive and have some tolerance in relation to his own shortcomings; for the 'ideal teacher' will always be felt to demand that the student be equally perfect, without blemish. Equally, it is of vital importance that the student who is provocative in his behaviour and expects to be punished, is able to put against his expectations of a punitive authority someone who in fact takes a firm but benign stand. It is equally important that the student who makes us feel worthless is not left with the triumph and guilt at having made us utterly despondent. Our example of courage in the face of difficulties will help him to struggle with his nastiness and go on working in spite of feelings of worthlessness.

In as far as powerful feelings are alive and active in the present, they are capable of change within the context of a new relationship. Thus the school at which the child spends such a large part of his waking life, and the teachers who become such influential adults for the student, have a great responsibility for providing experiences which will encourage trust, as opposed to idealisation and dread, and thus help the individual to grow. Here are two examples of how school experiences became woven into the history of individuals and part of their inner world.

(i) One of our course members told us that she had been extremely anxious that she might be late for our first meeting. When we talked about the roots of our feelings in childhood, she suddenly realised *why* she was so anxious. She recalled joining her secondary school a few days after the beginning of term. In spite of the fact that it was known that her absence from school had been unavoidable, she found herself teased by the school-mates and treated with harshness by the headmistress, as if it had been her fault that she had started late. When she forgot her gym-shoes on the second day this was cited as yet another example of her unreliability. When she was able to communicate her unhappiness to other girls they told her things would be better when their 'nice' form teacher returned. When Miss B came she was indeed very kind; she asked the girl about her family and the school she came from, and this made her feel that she was interested in her as a person and helped her to link her present experience with the past. The anxiety about being late for a new 'school' had remained buried and had been re-evoked when she joined the course.

(ii) A class had the misfortune to have three different form teachers within a year. It was a difficult class, containing a number of boys who were disruptive and uninterested in work. The headmistress noted how differently the pupils reacted to the changes. Some of them claimed that they didn't mind their teachers leaving. 'Good riddance,' they would say, 'she was no good anyway'; yet their attendance became more sporadic and their work deteriorated. Other pupils appeared upset and depressed and voiced their worry that they were so awful that no teacher could stand them.

At this point a senior teacher took over. The class only settled down when he assured them that he would stay with them for the rest of the year. He had intended to leave after a short period but, given the particular history of this class, felt he needed to stay on in order that the children could re-establish their belief in someone reliable and strong enough to deal with their difficulties. The pupils did in fact begin to work very much harder, trying to make up for what they thought had been their contribution to undermining their former teachers and making them leave. Being given plenty of warning about ending also enabled the children to talk about being left once again, and express their anger, disappointment, as well as their worry at not being good enough to be wanted by any teacher.

Chapter 3

Aspects of the teacher's relationship to the student

Introduction

Once we realise the crucial role the teacher plays in the mental and emotional life of students, it becomes essential to examine the attitudes and expectations he brings to the relationship. The teacher will be aware of some of these and not at all aware of others, yet they will all deeply colour the way he views (a) the nature of his role, (b) the way he perceives, interprets and responds to the students' behaviour, and (c) the way he expects to be regarded by them. His convictions will be based on his life experiences and what he has learnt from them. They will have developed on the basis of what he felt towards those responsible for his education (not only his teachers but members of his family and other mentors), the way he perceived their adult behaviour and how they set about the fulfilment of their task as educators. It will be of the utmost importance whether the teacher's attitudes are based primarily on an identification with the good qualities of parents and teachers and an appreciation of a child's difficulties and struggles; or alternatively, on the more unhelpful qualities of his parents and teachers and/or his own unsatisfied child-like desires. Let us consider the following statements made by student teachers in discussing their choice of career:

'I enjoyed school and liked my literature teacher in particular. He was enthusiastic about English, encouraged me to go on when I felt hopeless about my progress, but was strict when I was shirking work. I found him a great help and would like to become like him.'

'I hated school. I couldn't bear all the rules and disciplines. When I become a teacher, I want to let the children do just what they like and I will help them to rebel against anyone in authority.'

'I had a very strict upbringing. Self-control, doing what you were told and being punished if you did not obey were the order of the day, both at home and at my boarding school. I did not particularly like it, but I think it was good for me and I believe that this kind of discipline would do the kids of today a power of good.'

'My parents cared only about my academic achievements. I did well at school, but I became a blue-stocking and my social life suffered. I would like to show the students I teach that I don't only judge them on the basis of their work performance but that they matter as individuals.'

These comments show how much the aspiration of the student teachers derived from their identification with admired, respected or feared adults on the one hand, and their identification with children on the other. The teacher thus approaches the student with a dual perspective. He looks at the student from the point of view of an adult responsible for educating him; at the same time he has some awareness based on his own experiences of what it is like to be a child, an adolescent, a pupil and hence he has some preconceptions about the feelings which students may harbour towards adults and teachers. We should note further that it was the students' perception of the *nature of the relationship* between teacher and taught which shaped their concept of teaching and made them want to pass on to the next generation the kind of education they had had or, alternatively, wished they had received in the past.

The teacher's transference

The transference aspect of the teacher's relationship to students is therefore composed of various elements:

(1) His own childhood desires, wishes, fears, hate and love (compare previous chapter). This will enable him on the one hand to empathise with children but, on the other, it may also increase his anxiety; for instance, if his relationship to adults has been marked by powerfully envious feelings about their creative capacities, he will be afraid that the children he teaches will equally wish to attack and spoil his creativity as a teacher.

(2) The picture of adulthood which he has taken into his mind, e.g. strong, weak, fragile; adults having some privileges closely allied to responsibility, or adults free to follow their impulses without regard to others.

(3) The nature of the link between adult and child, e.g. adults purposely frustrating, suppressing and humiliating children or, alternatively,

caring for children, fostering their growth, respecting their individuality.

Not only do we have aspirations and fears that we know about, but we are also likely to carry into the situation attitudes unbeknown to us. The latter form part of the internal picture of relationships and will powerfully influence our perception and behaviour. We never completely outgrow infantile wishes and attitudes and they are bound to some extent to invade our private and intimate relationships. It is important, however, that we strive to become aware of them so as to minimise their interference in our professional life. We need to look critically at some of the aspirations as well as the fears with which teachers approach their task and go on to discuss some of the problems of which the teacher may be unaware. I would like to differentiate between the attitudes which foster mental/ emotional growth in students and those, which because they are based on the teacher's unworked-over childhood conflicts, are likely to undermine the students' development towards adulthood. We are bound to have shortcomings and all the aspects of behaviour described below will be true of most of us at certain times.

In addition, we are constantly exposed to pressure in our jobs and some situations and some students are likely to bring out the more adverse aspects of our natures. Yet it may be helpful to become aware of our individual bias and our weaknesses. This is not only important for the sake of our students, but it will also free us to find more adult satisfaction in our work. In the relationship between teacher and student the optimal one obtains when both partners benefit. Just as parents develop and enjoy the challenges that nurturing of their offspring entails, so the teacher can grow mentally and emotionally through the stimulus of meeting a variety of challenging students. Yet too often teachers find themselves feeling exhausted and depleted by the demands of their job and deeply dissatisfied with their performance. In other instances they themselves are guilty of exploiting the vulnerability and dependency of their pupils. We therefore need to examine our behaviour especially at those times when we feel either unduly anxious and burdened, or unduly virtuous about the performance of our task. Even the more painful and frustrating aspects of the work can become a subject of interest if we can find the space and tolerance to think about the problems we meet and be interested to know what we might learn from them.

Aspirations of the teacher

To pass on knowledge and skills

What characterises the teacher is his/her desire to communicate and pass on knowledge and skill to others. Knowledge, talent and skill may be regarded as precious gifts which one has been given and, in turn, wish others to benefit from. Some teachers expressed this by saying that they thought themselves to be so much better off than their pupils. They felt sorry at the helplessness of children who had not mastered similar skills, e.g. something as basic and essential to the acquisition of knowledge as the ability to read, write and count. Others longed to open up to their students those areas of thinking and experience which had enriched their own lives, like literature, science, the wonders of nature, or the ability to express oneself in one of the arts. This generous impulse to share with others is to be distinguished from a conviction that we must instruct students in what we consider to be 'appropriate', arrogantly assuming that we know what is 'good' for the pupil. Some teachers, for example, convey their belief that their subject, their particular area of expertise, their particular method or the theories they subscribe to are the only important or valid ones. This has less to do with an interest in the furtherance of knowledge, truth and beauty than a desire for disciples and inheritors. If students are forced to accept without questioning what they are taught, it will, in all but the most rebellious and independent students, stifle a spirit of enquiry, undermine individual effort and kill off a genuine desire for learning on the basis of experience.

Some exhibitionism, a common trait in teachers, is harmless. To some, however, it assumes a prime importance. A teacher may love to hear himself speak, show himself off and give a brilliant performance. He might indeed become the object of hero-worship, thus gaining the adoration he seeks, but in the process is likely to provoke a great deal of envy. The danger is that he may incline students to wish to adopt his style and take over his knowledge as a piece of equipment to give themselves power and status rather than lead them to develop an interest in the subject matter as such. In the long run, the more discerning pupils will become aware that the teacher is primarily concerned to boost his inflated self-image and does not have a real interest in promoting learning nor care much about the student as an individual. On the other hand, one of the hazards of teaching is the possibility of losing one's enthusiasm for the subject as well as the interest in how to convey it in a way that is helpful to any particular student. As a result of such lack of hopefulness teachers resort to repetition and mere drumming of information into their pupils' heads. Such teachers are likely to be boring and convey to their students that learning is a purely arduous, limited and unenterprising task.

To enable students to succeed

To help a student to reach a desired goal is part of the teacher's aim. Many teachers indeed derive great joy from their student's achievements. Added to the pleasure of seeing the progress is the satisfaction derived from having helped students to succeed. To help when needed, to enable the student to struggle with uncertainty, to encourage him to persist in the face of difficulties are all essential functions of the teacher. Such behaviour is to be distinguished from fostering a fiercely competitive attitude where examinations and marks for homework become the all-important measuring rod. Tests are then likely to be experienced by the students as a matter of beating their peers, being the first and best, better or worse than others, rather than reaching a required standard. A teacher exclusively interested in the number of passes and grades achieved by his class, is likely to encourage over-weaning ambition and rivalry between students rather than allowing them to take an interest in learning for its own sake and to be helpmates to each other. Sometimes the wish for success derives from the teacher's need to be seen to be successful, and this may drive him to make unreasonable demands on his students. Moreover, when they do well, they tend to be paraded as the product of his wonderful work rather than being allowed to earn praise in their own right. This kind of teacher is likely to lose interest in those pupils who are slow and do not greatly add to his reputation. He is also likely to be highly competitive with his colleagues, claiming and fighting that his subject or class be allotted the most gifted students, be the one most subscribed to, and be treated with special consideration.

To foster personal development

Most teachers see their job as extending well beyond teaching, they regard themselves as educators concerned to foster personal growth. In this respect they have a function very similar and complementary to that of parents. The attributes which our group of teachers considered to be desirable reflected this wish to be like good parental figures: to encourage and give confidence, to be tolerant, to be considerate, to be kind, to be consistent in one's discipline, to be interested in the student's welfare, to provide a structure which allows for experimentation as well as security. The corollary of this parental aspect of the relationship is that we come to experience our pupils very much as if they were our own children. This may be of benefit: our love and interest will make us watch over them with concern, worry about them and take pleasure in their progress. We should, however, carefully examine our internal picture of the nature of this parenting relationship and question how far our actions accord with our views: do we consider the parental function to be one of fostering development, or are we trying to mould children in our own image? Do we wish to impose our own standards on children or do we allow them to have different views, different aptitudes, different value systems from our own, to have space to develop their individuality? Are we providing a structure which enables those dependent on our services to grow into independent adults or is it designed to keep students in a child-like state? The latter may arise from an underestimation of the pupils' strength, an idea that they are such tender plants that they have to be 'molly-coddled'. More frequently, it stems from the teacher's need to have others permanently dependent on him. A teacher whose private life is unfulfilled may be especially at risk in this respect. He may shower attention and gifts on students in order to gain their love and become indispensable to them. He may get depressed during holidays and be disappointed when devotion and gratitude are not forthcoming. He may also become very possessive and subtly communicate jealousy of anyone (be they other class-teachers or friends of the student) who gains the respect and admiration of 'their' student.

Some teachers can never do enough for their students, spare no effort, or time. While devotion and a capacity for sacrifice is an essential parental quality, the teacher's giving-attitude may be prompted by a need to be seen as the 'ideal parent'. By over-indulging, over-feeding, over-teaching, the teacher may be putting himself forward as someone to be loved and may bask in admiration and self-idealisation. Far from helping his students' emotional growth, he is then in fact encouraging greed, passivity and parasitism in his students. His pupils are neither given the spur to struggle with inevitable frustrations nor the opportunity to develop self-reliance. Some teachers set themselves a perfectionist standard and implicitly convey that others should live up to this. Such perfectionism can be experienced as too harsh a demand and can be so far beyond the student's reach that it undermines his confidence of ever satisfying his teacher. The teacher becomes not only an outer but an inner model that it is impossible to live up to. Even the prospect of growing up may become a forbidding one if it involves having to be someone as 'perfect' as the apparently 'ideal' teacher.

To befriend students

Teachers of adolescents and young people will often see themselves in the role of a friend. They may proffer advice, provide companionship and some social facilities in their spare time. This is fine as long as the teacher is careful not to show favouritism. He needs also to consider whether he is giving more of his time and energy to any one pupil than he has realistically to offer, bearing in mind the needs of other students for whom he is responsible as well as his own need for recreation and privacy. The maternal/paternal caring functions of the teacher have to be distinguished from the behaviour which is of a more seductive nature and may even have a delinquent quality to it. Some teachers, for instance, pride themselves on being on the same level as their students, joining them in adolescent activities like drug-taking or smoking sessions. Most young people recognise this as the teacher's wish to regain his lost youth, or alternatively as an attempt to avoid being seen as someone in authority. Such behaviour may in fact be prompted by the teacher's fear of the hostility and anger which is likely to be directed towards anyone in such a position. He may choose to send his students to a senior colleague or the head of the school in order to avoid having to take disciplinary action. Yet such an evasion will soon be discovered to be cowardly and hypocritical for when it comes to examination or the eventual enforcement of disciplinary action, the teacher cannot avoid being identified with those who are in authority.

It is usual for the teacher to find some of his students physically attractive. Sexually seductive behaviour is a real danger which may occur in relation to children of any age, but is a special problem for those who are working with adolescents and young people. It is natural for youngsters to admire and have a temporary crush on a teacher. It is therefore most important to be mindful of the students' vulnerability to feel sexually attracted to their teacher and not to exploit the situation. We have to examine our own susceptibility to sexual feelings towards members of the same, as well as the opposite sex, and keep them under control. The teacher will have to be careful neither to behave seductively nor act in a manner that lends itself to being misunderstood by the students. Here is an example: A female student turned to her college tutor when she was in distress about her relationship with an older married man. In the course of trying to comfort her and sort out her problems, the tutor visited her man friend, told him off for his unkindness towards the student, took the student for drives in his car, and spent more and more time with her. All this was well meant but he was unaware that his behaviour encouraged the girl to think that he was not only taking a sympathetic interest in her problem but also putting himself forward as a more attractive companion than her previous man friend. The tutor felt both flattered and scared by the girl's attention and found it difficult to extricate himself from a relationship that had somewhat overstepped professional boundaries.

We have a responsibility to encourage the development of mature attitudes, to behave as adults capable of concern and thoughtfulness, taking responsibility for our actions, both in our relationships with individuals and groups of students. The opposite, namely yielding to childlike impulses, an atmosphere dominated by sensuousness and thoughtlessness, by envy and jealousy, is typical of adolescence. If the teacher takes cognizance of this, he will be on his guard not to be drawn into, nor stimulate, such tendencies further. It is all too easy to provoke excitement by vague promises of unrealistic possibilities and innuendos of secret forbidden adventures. All these can be subtly implied in word and gesture. The play 'The Prime of Miss Jean Brodie' portrayed graphically and tragically the dangers of this kind of interaction.

Fears of the teacher

Fear of criticism

Many teachers are afraid that they will be the target of critical comments from their students. They are of course justified in assuming that they will be the object of detailed scrutiny. Their academic ability, physical appearance and behaviour are likely to be closely studied, constantly appraised and critically reviewed. In this situation, the teacher's mistakes and weaknesses are unlikely to escape notice for long. It is, therefore, essential that he has some self-awareness and tolerance of his own shortcomings. It is equally important that he has enough confidence to be able to distinguish between critical comments which are justified and those that arise from spite and yet others which are a projection of the pupil's unwanted feelings. Most pupils respond with increased respect and concern to a teacher who can admit when he is in the wrong. Such truthfulness also encourages students to develop some tolerance towards themselves, to be honest in their self-appraisal and learn from their mistakes. Some teachers, however, become extremely apologetic and self-effacing about any little weakness or mishandling on their part. Pupils will soon become aware how easily they can hurt such teachers and undermine their confidence. Some students may abstain from criticism out of concern; others may be less able to exercise such restraint and become increasingly sadistic. More often the opposite attitude prevails, namely the teacher's wish to put himself above criticism. A teacher who experiences any adverse remark as an attack is likely to 'hit back' and adopt a severely critical attitude towards his students. His inability to stand any criticism or his demand that others be beyond reproach at all times, makes it hard for students to develop an honest and sincere relationship to him and to themselves.

Fear of hostility

Most people are afraid of hostility. This is partly due to the fact that it is almost invariably experienced as a personal attack. It is helpful to distinguish those instances where one is the object of hatred from others where students have enough confidence in the teacher's strength to trust him to understand and cope with their angry feelings.

Some frustration is inherent in learning and hence some measure of anger is likely to be part and parcel of the situation. A teacher who is afraid of this will avoid making demands on the student and be unable to face him with unpleasant facts. Not only is this likely to undermine the student's belief in the teacher's sincerity but an unrealistic appraisal of the student's work will prevent him from achieving the best he is capable of. In addition, students are bound to experience some degree of rivalry and envy in relation to adults who appear to be successful and creative in their professional and/or social life. The teacher who is frightened of the expression of anger and envy is merely trying to keep such feelings out of this particular relationship. The student is therefore forced to store up these negative feelings and express them elsewhere, either towards another teacher or someone outside the school. If there is no-one who will tolerate such feelings, it strengthens the student's fear that all aggression is destructive and so powerful that it cannot be dealt with by anyone. He may be driven to inhibit it to a degree where it interferes with outgoing-ness and achievement. On the other hand, a student less able to control his anger may become increasingly violent in the hope that someone will take him seriously and help him to deal with his aggression by setting limits.

Fear of losing control

A teacher is faced with managing many tense situations: between a pupil and himself, between the different members of a class and between the whole group and himself. He may be afraid of losing his temper, afraid that a disruptive pupil will interfere with the work of others, or that the whole group will get out of hand. Teachers tread a tight-rope between being too severe and restrictive or else too slack, allowing slovenliness and chaos to reign. It is often extremely difficult to allow enough freedom but remain in control. In spite of this, some teachers feel guilty at ever getting irritated and angry. It is only human to lose one's temper on occasion and usually this does less harm than one imagines. It may be possible subsequently to discuss with the class or individual why a particular piece of behaviour has got under one's skin. Some teachers are of the opinion that the only way to control children is to set very strict limits and deal out severe punishment at the slightest sign of disobedience. Indeed, punish-ment, even caning, is sometimes preferred by the pupils themselves because it 'wipes the slate clean'. Having received punishment, there is thought to be no need to give further attention to what has gone wrong or to suffer pangs of remorse. Yet it is just this possibility of thinking about the reason for their behaviour and how their actions affect others which could lead to understanding; eventually this might lead them to wish to make amends for harm done and help them to control their hurtful actions. Severely punitive teachers not only become brutalised themselves but they breed students who pass on the cruel treatment they have received to others who are younger and weaker than themselves. This will not be a matter of choice but rather the expression of an internalised harsh and cruel relationship.

A very different situation pertains where the teacher is afraid of warm and close relationships. He may be rather theoretical in his approach to students and adopt a cold, distant manner. One factor in this might be the teacher's fear that his sexual impulses will get out of control. Such anxiety can be very realistic and is to be respected. Another reason for keeping himself aloof might be the teacher's dread of getting over-burdened by his students' problems. If we are willing to be receptive to other people's feelings we put ourselves in the position where others unload their depression, their worry and their fears. We open ourselves to a whole flood of misery and tragedy in their personal and family life. Some teachers are afraid that they will be overwhelmed by such outpourings; others fear that they will become too deeply involved and will take on more than they or the student can cope with. They then find ways of avoiding contact by ensuring that there is no time available or by quickly fending off personal confidences with a ready piece of advice or a cheering remark. Others feel that having gained some knowledge about their students they will be called upon to intervene actively in the situation and change it. This is rarely the case. It is often quite enough for the teacher to listen to the student with sympathy and understanding and make himself available to the student's emotional pain. Such sharing of a burden is a great relief in itself – one that is usually very much underestimated. By providing a willing ear, he may have given the student some hope that there is someone prepared to listen and help bear painful feelings. If the needs of the student go beyond what the teacher can offer or is capable of managing, he can suggest someone else who is in the position to offer help.

Problems of which the teacher may be unaware

Hostility towards parents

There are adults who attribute all their shortcomings and misfortunes to their upbringing and hold their parents responsible for their difficulties. A teacher of this kind will tend to seek the reasons for the student's difficulty in his home and assume that the parents must be at fault, even when he has no first-hand knowledge about them. He will be easily drawn into criticising and blaming the parents, taking the pupil's accounts as statements of fact rather than the way the relationship is perceived by him.

Sometimes the parents are well known to the teacher and may indeed be very difficult people. Yet siding with the student against the parents is likely to strain family relationships still further. It is always easier to allot blame rather than examine the contributions the student has made to the situation, and encourage him to take responsibility for his actions. A hostile attitude to his parents will encourage the child and adolescent to get stuck in self-pity, become someone who wears a chip on his shoulder and bears a grudge against home and society at large. He may also wish to revenge himself on those whom he holds responsible for his misery. There is a great difference between accusing one's parents and being aware that they too have difficulties. They may have found it hard to grow into mature adults either because of their own endowment or because they did not have good enough parental care themselves.

Hostility of teachers towards the pupil's parents shows itself in many ways. For instance, they usually speak about 'sending for parents' who at the very least can be ordered to appear and at worst are regarded as delinquents who must appear at school in order to be told off. It is this kind of attitude which makes many parents reluctant to contact the school. They are terrified of being blamed or made to feel inadequate. Most parents are only too ready to feel guilty and inferior in relation to these 'high and mighty' teachers. They need to be encouraged to relate to teaching staff on a more equal, more adult basis. Of course, it may also be the teachers who are afraid of meeting the parents. Quite often they fear that they will be found to be not good enough for the parents to entrust them with their offspring. They may see in the pupil's parents an image of their own parents coming to check whether they are adequately grown-up to look after children, or are still children themselves simply playing at being mother or father.

Rivalry with parents

The unresolved competition with one's parents may be carried forward into adulthood. The teacher will then attempt to be a better mummy than Mummy or a better daddy than Daddy. This is usually based on arrogance and self-idealisation. If this attitude has a strong hold over the teacher it will stimulate him to compete with the parents of his pupils. He may want to show himself off as being cleverer, wiser, nicer, kinder, more permissive and exciting than the student's father and mother. This will encourage the student to retain a sharp division between idealised, wonderful teacher and hated, denigrated, terrible parent. In turn, this can undermine the struggle to learn to discriminate between good and bad qualities in each person, to tolerate the imperfections in others and integrate the different aspects of himself. Alternatively, the teacher's seductiveness may put the pupil into a painful conflict of loyalty between home and school. In order to protect his parents he may opt to turn against the teacher in a way that is bound to interfere with his capacity to learn.

It is not infrequent for a school to pride itself on providing the ideal environment for the upbringing of children. Educational institutions, moreover, often take the whole credit for a pupil's progress, devaluing, or even disregarding, the contribution made by the family in helping the child to develop. The idea that the pupil is the property of the school leads to strained relationships between teachers and parents and lack of co-operation. It is important that teachers and parents see themselves as carrying a joint responsibility for the development of the pupil and are able to help each other in this task. They have indeed a complementary role and need to share the joys and burdens of the child's education.

Identification with childish desires

Work with children and adolescents may stimulate the infantile aspects of our own personality. If the teacher has not sufficiently worked through these, he may become identified with the pupil's demand that all his desires should be fulfilled and endlessly gratified. The teacher may, for instance, agree that students need 'spoon-feeding' and thus be inclined to do most of the work for them. He may not realise that, in acceding to their infantile wishes, he is not only pampering them and undermining their innate capacities, but at the same time satisfying his own wish that learning should be easy. Equally, a teacher who has been, or longed to be, his parents' special child may gain vicarious satisfaction when he bestows special attention on his favourite pupil. (The rest of the class will have to suffer the pangs of jealousy which the teacher has never been able to cope with adequately.) These modes of behaviour encourage dependency and hamper students from coming to grips with reality. They will find that the outside world (senior school, place of employment, social partners) will treat them very differently from the way they have been led to expect by the infantilising teacher.

The inclination to indulge students may receive further reinforcement from the teacher's fear that any frustration will lead to an outburst of unlimited anger. If the teacher himself is inclined to react with violent rage to the absence of gratification, it will make him so frightened of his student's hostile attacks that he may be unable to enforce limits. The teacher's inability to help his students to struggle with frustration undermines their coming to grips with reality. It can be positively destructive if it leads him to promote escape routes from reality, like encouraging pupils to take drugs, to smoke or drink excessively.

Identification with destructive aspects of the students

We have seen that it is essential to growth that destructive impulses are at first separated off from constructive ones. If, however, polarisation remains extreme and the destructive parts of the personality are not eventually brought within the orbit of kindly control, they stay permanently separated off. When they surface they are treated as a foreign body, suppressed or disowned. The teacher in this state of mind is then likely to attribute bad qualities to others and fight them there, e.g. when he discovers signs of envy, jealousy, delinquency in his students, he is unable to muster any tolerance of such qualities and will be inclined to treat them with great harshness. Instead of helping his students to harness such tendencies by kindly but firm understanding, he is likely to resort to condemnation and punishment. Far from ameliorating the situation, it leaves destructive feelings festering and ready to assert themselves. In addition the student is likely to internalise the teacher's intolerant attitude. It may make him so ashamed and guilty that he is unable to take responsibility for his actions and feelings. He may even seek punishment or engage in self-punishment to avoid the pangs of too severe a conscience or, alternatively, he may try to escape and rebel against such external/ internal strictures by acts of violence.

Rivalry and envy of younger siblings

To some extent children, adolescents and adults younger than ourselves will be experienced as younger brothers and sisters competing for attention and admiration, while those senior to us may be thought of as older siblings. Those who have not had brothers and sisters are just as prone to react in that way. They have the further handicap of not having had the opportunity to work through their feelings of jealousy and envy toward the 'baby' or the older children in the family. Insufficient integration of rivalrous feelings can seriously interfere with the way the teacher deals with students. If for example he finds jealousy unacceptable, he may be blind to its manifestation (like parents who claim that their older child is *never* jealous of the baby), leaving the pupils to deal with it themselves. He may be unable to cope with their competition for attention, and may overlook younger or less able students becoming the objects of bullying attacks. If he is identified with the jealous older sibling he may himself adopt a tyrannical attitude towards his students or agree that younger children are to be 'underdogs'. Alternatively, he may be so frightened of the jealousy of the older ones that he does not enable new students to find their place amongst the established members of the class.

If the teacher is inclined to be envious it may show itself in an attitude which is summed up by saying: what was good enough for me is good enough for them – why should they have it easier? He may be envious of particular qualities, e.g. physical attractiveness, youthfulness, enthusiasm, intellectual or artistic abilities. The envious teacher will try to suppress the emergence of real talent. Alternatively, he may be helpful to his gifted students so long as they are not as yet real competitors as good as himself or able to surpass his own achievement. At the point of success, however, he is likely to discourage students in a subtle way, e.g. by pointing out their shortcomings or implying that they are not really 'there' yet; he may also stand in the way of his students' opportunities to prove themselves and gain wider recognition. Such inclinations will, of course, also show themselves in his attitude towards other teachers. He is likely to stress their faults rather than their good qualities and hope to undermine the students' attachment and admiration for the colleagues he envies.

Chapter 4

Emotional aspects of learning

In the previous chapters we have traced some of the hopes and fears that attach themselves to the person in the role of teacher or student. Now we shall turn our attention to the process of learning as such. We shall go on to discuss the teacher's function in providing and maintaining an attitude of mind which facilitates learning. Learning is the specific task for which students and teachers come together. It is a highly complex task, not only because of the inherent complexity of any subject studied but because of the emotions aroused by the learning situation itself.

Learning and mental pain

Let us observe young children in a nursery school trying to use a set of bricks to build a tower. A little boy puts bricks on top of each other but they soon crash down. Encouraged by his teacher to arrange them more carefully, he tries again. He becomes excited by his success and piles on more and more bricks until they come tumbling down. Different children will react to this situation in different ways. Robert, at this point, begins to cry, and presently turns to other toys in a desultory manner. Michael, at his next attempt at constructing a tower, deliberately hits it before it collapses. It looks as if he had meant the bricks to fall down by his own volition rather than acknowledge that he is not yet able to achieve what he had set out to do. When, on another occasion, they do fall down of their own accord, he bangs the bricks against each other and angrily flings them across the room. Timothy, after his initial efforts have failed, takes more care to study the size and position of the bricks until eventually, after many repeated attempts, he manages to balance a number of them on top of each other.

We can imagine the kind of school reports that might be given to these children later on if their behaviour remains similar to that observed in the nursery. Robert might be said to give up easily, get frustrated and distracted. Michael's school books are described as messy because he keeps crossing out whatever is not perfect; he is said to not be able to bear criticism and often becomes aggressive when things don't go his way. Timothy is reported to be able to show good concentration, to be thorough and persistent in his work. The crucial difference between these children is the way they react to the lack of success which is bound to occur when struggling to acquire a skill. Robert becomes despairing, Michael controlling and angry, while Timothy is able to use the experience to become more curious about the nature of the objects he is playing with and their relationship to one another. Putting it a different way, we might say that Timothy is able to find within himself resources of hope which enable him to work at a problem, while the other children are overcome by their feelings of frustration and helplessness. While Robert tries to escape such feelings by abandoning the task, Michael tries to manipulate the situation into one where he can feel in control. Learning arises in a situation in which we do not as yet know or are as yet unable to achieve what we aim to do. It thus invariably involves uncertainty, some degree of frustration and disappointment. This experience is a painful one and if it is more than can be tolerated then it may be evaded, as in the case of Robert, or else dealt with omnipotently and angrily as in the case of Michael.

While our behaviour becomes more sophisticated as we grow older, the fundamental attitudes of adults when faced with difficult learning situations remain very similar to the ones described. We try to avoid having to struggle with uncertainty, yearn for simple answers, become angry when frustrated and easily give up the struggle. Let us listen to members of the teachers' course on the occasion of their third meeting with me. I find that the 'honeymoon' period tends to be over by the second or at the latest third evening. The group is by then beginning to face the reality of what the course provides and the complexity of the subject they have come to study. Frustration and disappointment now come to the fore. It is expressed in statements like the following:

'All this is very interesting but what I want to know is how to manage disruptive pupils in my class – when are you going to talk about that?'

'Our task as educators is to straighten out problem-children and I would like you to tell me just how to do that.'

'We have children from all sorts of different backgrounds – I'd like to know how we can change the families of these children.'

'I find my job gets on top of me, I'm considering leaving – when the class gets rowdy I just give up and let them get on with fighting each other or send the noisy ones to the headmaster.'

'I want to be patient and kind, but I do lose my temper some of the time – I'd like to know why I get so upset and irritated by some of the kids.'

So here is one lone voice trying to ask *why* and trying to understand what is going on – while most of the group seem to want to rush into precipitate action. When I point out that we first need to understand the meaning of the children's behaviour, the complaints become more and more forceful, like 'I haven't heard you say anything yet that is of immediate practical help to me in managing an attention-seeking child.' As if to convince me that a quick solution rather than understanding the nature of relationships is required, I am given a number of examples of extremely difficult children and worrying situations that the teachers have to cope with: violent, suicidal, delinquent adolescents, children unwilling or unable to learn, children constantly demanding attention from the teacher. Some of them are pathetic, some of them deprived, others are felt to be purely a nuisance. Not only are teachers troubled by their classes but they find themselves also the object of demands made by the parents (and by themselves) that they should be totally responsible for turning the children into mature human beings, change them in some magical way. In addition they feel pressurised by the demands of society which decrees that children attend school for a prescribed number of years, although some of them wish to leave earlier. There are the requirements of the Examination Boards for Higher Education which impose a strict curriculum on the teacher and the achievement of an academic standard with which children have to comply.

Listening to the teachers, I become aware that what has driven them to attend my course is the pressure of anxiety about their role and that they have come in the hope of obtaining quick relief for the painful situation in which they find themselves. They are looking for instructions about what to do, wishing to learn *about* human beings, rather than from actual experience *of* others, afraid that their students and their own feelings will get out of control if they stop to look, listen and think. The lone voice trying to explore the nature of the learning/teaching relationship and asking 'why do I feel like this, when children behave in a certain way?', which might lead us to discover how we might help particular children, seems to have got lost in the medley of voices which are pressing for immediate answers, for some way of manipulating and controlling the 'bricks' of human experience with which they are faced. In fact, the more I look at the group in front of me, the more I become aware how much they mirror, albeit to a very mild degree, a group of classroom children. The group is restless, some people look bored, others have come late, one person asks to be excused, someone is scribbling, two are talking, some openly express their anger with me. One person calls me 'Mrs Windyberg', apparently by mistake, and a titter goes round the room. At this some members empathise with me as the teacher who has to put up with ridicule as well as discontent and disruptions. Someone says 'I wonder how *you* feel. I find that when people are hostile to me it makes me feel absolutely demolished.'

I had in fact been examining my thoughts during the foregoing discussion and I am reproducing them here because I think they throw light on the nature and strength of the pressures that can be exerted on teachers. Such self-observation might help us to understand the powerful dynamic forces at work and the strain on the teacher who resists being propelled into precipitate action, rather than helping his students to think about the observable facts and what might be learnt from them. Let me describe the series of emotional states that I underwent: the first was an increasing and compelling pressure to supply something that would meet the group's demands, such as providing instant answers to the questions raised. I felt pushed to produce information and exact lines of conduct which would solve the teachers' problems (and my problems with the teachers' group). It seemed that otherwise the situation would dissolve into chaos and I would lose control of the group. While I was aware that I could not provide a universal recipe for dealing with all kinds of disturbing phenomena, I nevertheless felt urged to at least give a brilliant theoretical exposition which would explain human behaviour. It would have been nice to do a trapeze act, to lift myself upon the slim rope of omnipotence to the heights of mental acrobatics, supported by the breathless admiration and acclaim of my audience.

Yet the more I searched my mind the more anxious I became at not being able to rise to the height of performance expected of me. Nothing I knew or could do seemed to come anywhere near to what was asked of me. I thought briefly of the books I had read, of other people's inspiring lectures, and how these might be utilised for next week's meeting – provided I could get away with my poor performance this time! At this point I found myself inwardly agreeing with those who thought me totally useless unless I did what I was asked to do, even something of a fraud at having put on a course without having the wherewithal to carry it through. I began to wonder whether I shouldn't ask someone else to take over the group for the next few evenings, someone more adequate to meet the requirements. Thus I went through a spiral of trying to be the ideal the group demanded, followed by a collapse into a total feeling of inadequacy, and ultimately a wish to escape from such an unpleasant experience. These feelings were all very real, involving alarm, panic and despair.

It was hard to hold on to the idea that, however great my limitations, I had *something* to offer which could help us in understanding the teachers' dilemma, namely some knowledge and experience of observing behaviour and thinking about the meaning of it. This also included the observation of the emotional impact others had on myself and using this as a valuable clue to understanding the nature of the relationship. This realisation enabled me to call a halt to wishing to run away or fall in with the group's demands. It made it possible to find enough space to think about the present experience and to be curious about what was happening between the members of the group and myself. The feelings evoked in me and the observation I was making of the group now became the focus of my study. I still felt rather lost as if travelling in an unknown area, but at least I had some equipment whereby I could begin to orientate myself. Gradually the meaning of the facts of the situation began to fall into place. I realised that I was being made to have some of the painful feelings that teachers experience in the course of their work. The members' behaviour, the way they talked and acted, as well as the more unfathomable, threateningly-charged atmosphere, were ways of communicating to me, letting me know how difficult it is to hold on to one's knowledge and thinking capacity in the face of a group of pupils who are demanding, impatient and aggressive when faced with the uncertainty and frustration which are inherent in learning; how undermining it is to face criticism and derision, how demoralising to be met by boredom and rejection, how frightening to be threatened with chaos and violence. All these hidden forces might be let loose if the teacher does not fit in with the wishes of the students. In this way my group of teachers were saying to me: 'this is what we have to put up with every day, let's see how you cope with a difficult class!' I do not wish to imply that this was done in a deliberate way, nor as a result of a conscious decision on their part – they were simply re-enacting in their relationship with me (transferring) the painful situation which they carried within themselves as a result of their own experiences. All these painful feelings were communicated to me in this most immediate and highly effective manner. It was a test of my capacity to withstand such anxieties and go on thinking, rather than falling into despair, evading the task or reacting by adopting a rigid system of teaching and controlling the group. They were presenting both what they had to deal with as teachers and demonstrating their own difficulties in finding themselves in a learning situation on the course. We thus had the opportunity of learning about the nature of the anxieties which beset the learner: fear of confusion and chaos in the face of unsorted 'bricks' of experience, helplessness in the face of not knowing, fear of inadequacy, fear of being judged stupid in comparison with others. At the same time we could observe how such anxieties propel the learner to grasp for quick solutions or demand answers from the teacher so as to be able to put an end to such anxieties. Even where simple answers can be given, the reliance on these tends to squash curiosity and experimentation and hence the development of exploration and thinking about data.

We also saw that the pain experienced by the learner, when intolerable, is got rid of into the teacher. If he is receptive to this he becomes the one who feels inadequate, frightened, stupid, helpless, confused, and he in turn may try to escape from this in a number of ways. He may meet fear of his ignorance about the world by a dazzling display of theoretical knowledge, fear of impotence by exerting power, fear of chaos by a rigid approach to his subject and a rigid control of his pupils, fear of inadequacy and humiliation by claiming superiority and making his students feel small. A vicious circle may be set up in which the teacher reacts to the powerful emotions evoked in him by helping the student to evade inevitable stress or forcing the anxiety back into him. These *are* quick solutions to the problem of mental pain, but in as far as they avoid the inevitable anxieties connected with learning, such a teacher is in fact discouraging the development of a capacity to think.

Real learning and discovery can only take place when a state of not knowing can be borne long enough to enable all the data gathered by the senses to be taken in and explored until some meaningful pattern emerges. The poet John Keats speaks about this capacity to bear 'uncertainties and doubts without irritable reaching after fact and reason', calling this 'negative capability'. If we are to understand other human beings, we have to start from a state of not knowing, an interest in finding out by observing, listening and being receptive to the communications conveyed by others to us, both verbally and non-verbally. We will try to rid ourselves of preconceptions whether they be about child-development and child-rearing, theories of human behaviour and attempt to ignore what we have learned about an individual by hearsay. It is important that we do not deal with our uncertainty by trying to explain our student's behaviour in terms of either his inborn bad character or bad environment. All such preconceptions are likely to make us blind and deaf to what we can actually discover on the basis of our own experience. If we are receptive and open-minded we shall find that we become the recipient of quite powerful feelings put (projected) into us. We may also find ourselves able to be curious about the nature of the feelings evoked in us and what they tell us about what is going on in the relationship.

The containment of pain and learning from experience

These are subjects which were central to the work of the psycho-analysts Melanie Klein and Wilfred Bion. In his analytic work with individuals and groups Dr Bion became aware that he was made to feel that part of the personality which the individual or group found too painful to bear. Some people will dump their problems into another person, wishing simply to get rid of them. Having used the other person as an emotional dustbin they may become afraid of him (for fear that he will push the rubbish back), or treat him with contempt as if he now had become rubbish. Others, however, use a receptive adult to communicate their distress in the hope that it might be understood and they might be helped to bear it. Bion states that the phenomena of being able to engender feelings in another person is convincingly explained by Melanie Klein's theory of projective identification, namely that there exists a phantasy that it is possible to split off part of one's personality and put it into another person. This mental mechanism, he says, is used either for communicating or for getting rid of a part of the personality which causes anxiety and conflict. Not only does the mechanism operate in phantasy, it results in modes of behaviour and action which in actuality evoke the desired response from a receptive person. He believed that from the beginning of life the baby is capable of acting in a way that engenders in the mother feelings that he does not wish to have or which he wants her to have. This behaviour also enables the mother to understand her baby and thus respond to him in accordance with his needs. Such receptiveness to another person's communication depends on the adult being in touch with feelings. A lack of awareness of feelings in any particular area would lead one to overlook relevant clues or to a distorted perception of them. On the other hand, receptivity to anxiety but an intolerance of such a state may leave the person overwhelmed by the feelings projected into him.

This way of looking at an interaction is enlightening in as far as it makes us aware that the effect a student or group of students has on us may be a valuable indication of the kind of feelings they want us to have. These may be ones of being idealised and admired and all sorts of positive aspects of a relationship, but more often what is deposited in us are the feelings the other one cannot bear or cannot bear on his own, such as helplessness, confusion, panic, guilt, despair or depression. He may need another person to help him with them. If such painful emotions can be received by another and understood it allows for growth and development for it gives hope that they can be looked at and borne. This is the role that a good mother performs for her child. D.W. Winnicott drew attention to the need of an infant to be held both physically and emotionally by the mother in order to facilitate his psychic development. It allows a time-span in which he can learn to cope with his anxiety.

Klein's understanding of the complex mental life of the infant, his limited ability to contain the destructive element of his nature and hence his need for a mother into whom he can project aggression and anxiety have clarified the emotional content of this holding function. Klein stated that the mother who can bear the pain put into her without becoming overwhelmed, acts as a container for the feared emotion. If she goes on responding lovingly to him, this conveys to him that there is someone capable of holding this feared part of himself without going to pieces. The child, finding his anxiety, aggression and despair accepted and contained, is enabled at a feeling level to realise that someone capable of living with a feared or rejected aspect of himself does in fact exist. Thus these parts of himself are felt to be not all-powerful and therefore they become less frightening; they are felt to be capable of being bound by love and concern.In this way they become divested of their most painful aspect. Anxiety having been modulated, the infant is able to internalise a kind of container-mother, holding this aspect of himself and thereby his internal world becomes more manageable and enriched.

W.R. Bion added to the parental function of acting as a container, that of a thinker; namely, a parent who has a capacity not only to care and worry, but to think about and clarify and differentiate between kinds of feelings. He states that the mother's imaginative reflection which he termed 'reverie' enables her to bring together the different elements of his experience into meaningful conjunctions. He distinguishes between thoughts and a thinker. The infant at an early stage is able to have phantasies associated with his physical experiences, a kind of primitive thought process. However, in as far as his phantasies become over-whelmingly painful, confusing and unmanageable, he evacuates them. It is the parental function to not only tolerate but sort out the nature of the experience, to digest it mentally and give it meaning, to be a thinker. If this happens the infant internalises not only a container of feelings but a mind that can hold thoughts. The person who has repeated experiences of his distress being understood and detoxified by another can thus gradually come to contain more emotional pain, find it less totally overwhelming and be able to think about his experience. On the other hand, if the infant consistently has experiences of his feelings being uncomprehended, he will take back into himself an experience of the anxiety being vast, unbounded, or 'nameless dread', as Bion called it. The infant's psyche, unable to deal with the burden of meaningless anxiety, is forced to expel feelings and phantasies more and more, and thus remain mindless.

The formulations that Klein and Bion have given us are of the greatest significance in understanding the emotional component in the process of all learning. The task of the teacher may be thought of as resembling the parental function: that is, to act as a temporary container for the excessive anxiety of his students at points of stress. It will mean that he will experience in himself some of the mental pain connected with learning, and yet set an example of maintaining curiosity in the face of chaos, love of truth in the face of terror of the unknown, and hope in the face of despair. If he is able to do this he is providing the conditions which will foster in the student an ability to tolerate the uncertainties connected with learning. Bion's formulation of mental life and interaction leads on to the idea that learning is at its best an on-going and mutual process. The pupil's ideas and thoughts are aided by a teacher who assists him in ordering them, particularly at such times when the learner becomes overwhelmed by too much undigested knowledge. The teacher's capacity to be reflective and thoughtful about data rather than producing ready answers enables the learner to internalise a thinking person. He in turn will produce new conjunctions of thoughts and meaning which may set off in the teacher a new combination of thinking about his subject. If we can remain open to each new student, each new class, and able to explore the not yet known, the triad of student, teacher and subject will become an extremely challenging and exciting experience from which we can go on constantly learning – analogous to the enriching learning opportunity that children provide for their parents.

Helpful interactions

Let us consider in greater detail the different elements in this helpful interaction between two people.

Attention and observation

What is needed in the first place is the willingness to pay attention; to listen and look and use all our senses to apprehend what is being communicated. Every detail of behaviour is potentially meaningful: a person's posture, his gait, the way he dresses, his facial expression, his voice, the way he talks as well as what he says or does not say. All of these tell us something about the nature of his relationship and the state of his mind. It is difficult for a teacher to observe in a large group, but over a period of time he may be able to take note, not only of the group as a whole, but also notice aspects of the behaviour of each of the children in his class. Often the teacher is aware of far more than he realises, and discussions with others frequently elicits information stored at the back of his mind. It might also stimulate him to pay more attention to facets of the student's behaviour when he meets him again. The child who gives no trouble and sits quietly in the corner, depressed or withdrawn, may need to be considered and require help as urgently or more urgently than the one who causes a commotion.

Be here Now

Openness and receptiveness

We know from our everyday experience that we can be affected by other people's moods. We may feel weighed down and enveloped by the depression of another person, or be infected by the gaiety and laughter of a group. The very words we choose suggest that we think of emotional states as being concretely transferable, getting right into us and taking us over. To some extent such feelings pass unseen like an electric current and we only know about them by the effect they have upon us. We usually do not talk about how others make us feel for fear that our reactions are irrational and simply the result of some personal weakness. This is to underrate the highly dynamic nature of mental states and relationships. Once the teachers' group came to realise that their feeling response could provide an important clue to the understanding of others, they were able to take much more note of which students made them irritated, who made them angry, depressed, unable to think, and those who made them feel flattered. It is of course essential that we check our emotional feeling responses against observable data. We may also need to compare our observations with those of others, as a safeguard against the danger that we are putting too much of ourselves into a situation, rather than responding to what has been communicated to us on a verbal or non-verbal level. These matters are seldom discussed in teachers' Common Rooms. When they are, it often results in a joining up against a student, blaming him or writing him off as impossible, rather than using the information available for the purpose of understanding the problem and as a basis for management decisions.

Awareness that we may be used as containers for excessive mental pain may make us more open and receptive to the communication of emotions. We may, on the other hand, be quite frightened to lay ourselves open to being filled up with feeling states that others find too intolerable to bear on their own. Often we are simply too preoccupied with our own troubles and find it quite hard enough to struggle with those without wishing to take on board the problems that others may burden us with.

Having an emotional experience

If we are open to receiving fear, depression, confusion, etc., we must be prepared to *have* an emotional experience. Furthermore, such empathy will evoke in us some of the anxieties we have experienced in similar situations in our childhood or our present life situation. The strength of the reverberations in ourselves will depend on whether they hit a particular vulnerable spot within ourselves, and also on the strength with which the painful emotions are projected by the other person. As it is part of the process that the feelings should get right under our skin, we must not be surprised if we sometimes feel overtaken by them and have to do hard mental work in order not to be overwhelmed. There is, on the other hand, no virtue in being a sponge-like absorber of painful emotions, becoming a martyr who takes upon himself all the suffering of the world. This only makes one an object of exploitation, a dustbin, and prevents one from helping the student to face and grapple with a painful conflict.

Thinking about the experience

What makes the painful experience bearable is an interest and ability to think about the feelings evoked in us. We may need space and time to *(Park Time)* consider the nature of the pain and appreciate what it is about. This thinking about feelings enables us both to have the experience and to apprehend its meaning, and may thus result in a better understanding of ourselves and others. It may lead to personal growth as well as a greater ability to tolerate the emotional pain of others.

Verbal or non-verbal communication or action

On the basis of understanding the meaning of a communication, it becomes possible to respond in a helpful way. We may act more appropriately or resist being drawn into action; or we may say something about what is going on in the relationship that embodies the truth of the emotional experience. In all these cases the other person will have an experience of emotional pain modulated by the understanding it has received, and this may make it more possible for him to eventually integrate it. On the basis of many such experiences in the classroom, students may develop a greater tolerance and capacity to bear emotional pain.

Unhelpful interactions

Non-attentiveness

We are often so preoccupied with ourselves or our activities that we do not pay enough attention to observing others. One may be blind or deaf to the communication that is being made, or we may perceive but not take any notice of it. An example may serve to illustrate this : 4-year-old Paul has been scribbling on a piece of paper but then smears ink on the table. After a while he throws his pen at another boy, then another one at the wall. The nursery teacher is too busy to notice. Presently he flings himself on to the floor, screaming and kicking. We might look upon Paul's increasingly uncontrolled behaviour as a means of expressing his inability to contain destructive feelings. He seems to try to make his need felt but as no one heeds him, he increasingly becomes more violent and out of control, culminating in a temper tantrum – an indication of his feeling totally overwhelmed. It is only when the teacher finally comes to his aid by talking to him and holding him physically that he calms down. Here is another example: an adolescent girl of 14 had been experimenting with

63

drugs. She was at times very sleepy, at times over-active, yet her parents did not notice. There were a number of telephone calls from members of her drug-taking group and she spoke quite loudly to them within the hearing of her parents. They, however, were afraid to interfere. When, after a while, she feared that she might become addicted, she burst into the parents' room one day and said, 'Why don't you stop me – don't you care at all?' Sometimes such adolescents do not give us the chance to know that they experience our inattentiveness to the indirect calls for help as lack of concern and understanding. They may become delinquent or violent and eventually involve the police or other authority figures in order to make known their urgent need for help in controlling their impulses.

Excessive permissiveness

Some adults feel that they are being very tolerant by allowing a child to behave in a destructive, cruel or exploitative manner. Such permissiveness is unhelpful. Far from reassuring the pupil, the teacher who puts up with tyrannical behaviour either towards himself or another child, conveys that he agrees with it or else is too frightened to set limits. Many people in the caring professions too readily pride themselves on being kind and giving when in fact their too ready acceptance of nastiness, greed and sloth encourages irresponsibility. They often do not recognise that the person may be troubled by his uncontrolled behaviour and that the teacher's failure to set limits leaves the pupil to cope with his destructive feelings all by himself. When the teacher does set limits and boundaries, this usually brings great relief.

Reacting

When the feelings projected into us take us over, we may attempt to get rid of them, and repay in kind. Thus we may react to rejection by becoming rejecting, to being terrified by terrorising, to despair by running away and avoidance. If we find ourselves afraid and weighed down by another person's emotions, we are inclined to react by denial, e.g. meeting depression by jollying the person out of it, rejection by placation, fear by pretending there is nothing to be afraid of. All these ways of behaving convey that such feelings are indeed unacceptable and unbearable. It may encourage the other person therefore to have to go on denying, inhibiting or repressing them. If he has enough hope he may attempt to use the next person as the container of such feeling states. Those teachers who are better able to tolerate painful emotions may therefore become the recipients of those negative attitudes which the student has not been able to express towards some of the other teachers.

Projection of pain into the dependent person

The worst situation occurs where the teacher (or other helper/parent) uses the student (or child/dependent person) as the container of his own unbearable feelings. Examples are the following: a teacher, intolerant of his own envy, may set about evoking envy in his pupil. A terrified teacher may tell horror stories to the children, filling up their minds with fear, dread and pessimism. Less hurtful but all the same serious: a teacher's intolerance of his own dependency may lead him to make his students unnecessarily dependent on him, or keep them in a dependent state for too long; a teacher unable to bear jealousy may provoke jealousy by always having a favourite pupil. A teacher seeing the pupil as the embodiment of all his own negative qualities and might treat him with hatred. All these situations make it extremely hard for the student to grapple with his own problems. He has in fact then to deal with a double dose of pain. Some students may simply avoid such teachers, others may have less chance to escape or be too weak to do so.

The basis of learning in infancy

In order to understand how some pupils, like Timothy, have acquired an ability to struggle with difficulties inherent in learning while others have not, we need to turn our attention to the emotional development in infancy and childhood. The amount of learning that has taken place before a child comes to school is immense. He will have had countless experiences of negotiating difficult situations and be helped with them or alternatively exposed to more than he could bear. We come to learn about ourselves and our environment through our sensory perception. We do not as yet know how much of the physical/emotional stress of the mother is conveyed to the foetus in utero. It is certain, however, that the newborn experiences an onslaught on his sensory apparatus. From having been in a warm environment, he finds himself suddenly propelled into the cold, from being enveloped he is exposed on all sides; he emerges from the dark into bright light, from a world of muted sounds to one full of noise; from being nourished automatically to having to make contact with an object outside himself for the source of food. The French doctor, Leboyer, has demonstrated how this dramatic experience can be made less traumatic by trying to recreate as much of the internal conditions as possible – this includes providing physical contact by putting the baby on the mother's stomach before the cord is cut, putting him to the breast as soon as possible, immersing the newborn in a warm bath and gently massaging him. It is fascinating to watch on film how this reduces the fearful cry of the newborn, enables him to gradually relax and begin to explore the world around him. It would appear that finding the impact of this new environment not too overwhelming, he can begin to be curious and initiate contact with it. It is of great importance that the mother goes on introducing the world into the baby's life 'in small doses' as Dr Winnicott put it. If changes are too abrupt or too frequent, or his experiences too painful, the infant responds with fear and eventual withdrawal. This may be only a temporary state of affairs but if the world is found to be too frightening and painful it may inhibit his curiosity and hence his capacity to learn. In extreme cases he may turn away from contact with others altogether. Whenever the 'bricks' of experience are found to be too overwhelming, we attempt to shut out the painful experience by withdrawing interest or trying to control the situation. On the other hand, a mother who continues after a few months to supply the infant's every need without his having to call out for help, becomes a mere adjunct of the baby and this may stop him from developing his motor, speech and mental abilities. It is also a worrying observation that some children who are full of questions up to the point of entering school, suddenly seem to have their curiosity stunted. Could it be that the child is presented with such an array of knowledge to be acquired that he finds it overwhelming? Or do the teaching methods employed discourage finding out by exploration and experimentation?

To return to the infant: at first his tolerance to frustration and pain is extremely limited. As he has as yet no sense of time each happening represents a totality and hence the infant's distress quickly becomes overwhelming. We can see a baby passing from one moment to the next, from a state of bliss to one when he seems to go to pieces, screaming, kicking and trembling. This makes it so important that at first his mother responds quickly to his need to be picked up, held securely, comforted or fed. She may, however, find that the screaming infant is unable to take the breast and turns away from it. A mother, uncertain of the goodness of her breast and the correctness of her handling, may feel affronted and either be angry with the baby or push the nipple into his mouth as if to prove that this is what he wants. A mother who is more sure of herself may be able to tolerate the baby's rejection, treat him gently and thus allow his fears and anger to be ameliorated. She thus allows him time to re-establish a good relationship before he is put to the breast. While in the first example the infant may feel that something undesired and painful is being forced into him (which adds to his fear of a bad mother), he has in the second instance an experience of bad feelings being taken away by a good mother. His experiences are physical and emotional – or psychosomatic. Some mothers will proffer the breast whenever the child cries, while most will soon discover that the child does not always wish to be fed but can be comforted by being carried about or gently rocked and sung to when he is frightened or miserable. The parents' physical handling expresses their understanding of how the infant feels. Hearing the child's cry and observing his behaviour, father and mother come to sense the nature of his distress – whether he is in a panic, furious at being left waiting, or despairing at help not being readily forthcoming. Their response in terms of apprehending the meaning of his communication helps him to sort out his experiences. A parent who can be in touch with the baby's terror, yet not too panicked by it, will be able to carry the baby in a way that will convey to him at a feeling level that terror can be borne, that someone exists who can hold such feelings without going to pieces. The opposite may, however, happen. A mother who quickly becomes terrified herself will not be able to stand the baby's anxiety – she may put him out of reach of hearing or deal harshly with him, trying, for example, to shake him in an attempt to stop the crying. This leaves the infant in a state of unrelieved panic, and eventually in a state of hopelessness which will lead him to turn away from the external world. Probably most infants will at some time or other suffer such traumatic experiences; it is only if the child repeatedly finds no relief for his distress that his development is likely to be seriously interfered with.

It would seem that the infant's good and bad experiences are at first very sharply divided in his mind. He tends to identify himself with the good aspects of his mother and to project the more destructive elements of his nature because they are too frightening and overwhelming to bear inside him. His phantasies are equally extreme and they are confirmed or alleviated by the kind of experience he has. Let us consider a baby gripping the breast hard. A mother, frightened of her baby's aggression, may pull her breast away, conveying to the infant that even a little aggression is hurtful and dangerous, and that she is too fragile to bear it and this may lead to inhibitions. Parents who are unable to set limits to aggressive behaviour are giving credence to the child's phantasy that his destructiveness is limitless and uncontrollable, hence he is likely to become more terrified. Eventually this leads to feeling so guilty that he cannot accept any responsibility for the harm he inflicts and this may result in increased aggressiveness. On the other hand, a mother who is less frightened of her baby's anger can help him sort out what is just a nip that is bearable from actions that hurt and those which actually do damage. In this way the handling of the parent is crucial in helping the child to differentiate between omnipotent phantasy and reality. If his destructive phantasies and fears are lessened by his experiences with his parents, it becomes possible for him eventually to take responsibility for his actions; to feel worry and concern for inflicting pain and being too much of a burden for those he loves and depends on. A child may then become more sparing of the other person and begin to allow the parents freedom to lead a life not centred on himself, and to show gratitude for having been given so much by making use of what he has received. It leads, in short to work, responsibility and creativity of all kinds.

Development is not conceived of as proceeding in a straight line. Even if we manage to attain the 'stage of concern' as Winnicott aptly called it, we tend to constantly go backwards and forwards between states of mind where we feel primarily frightened, persecuted, aggrieved, complaining and bearing a grudge against those who do not provide for us in the way we would wish – or primarily caring, appreciative of others and taking responsibility for our contribution to the difficult situations in which we find ourselves.

The struggle to maintain love and care in the face of anger, jealousy and envy, arises at every point of frustration and loss. The way we manage and are helped to manage such situations in infancy and childhood will deeply influence the capacity to do so later on in life. Some frustration is inevitable in any human relationship and if it is not excessive it is in fact a spur to development. How much frustration any particular child can deal with at any point in life is a matter of delicate parental judgment. One would not of course purposely frustrate a child but some parents bend over backwards trying to spare the baby (and/or themselves) any painful experience and indulge every whim of their offspring and thus become his slaves. Others readily proffer substitute comforters in the form of sweets, dummies or toys in order to avoid emotional upsets. A child may wish to adopt the inanimate object that is ever present and sensually satisfying rather than depend on a mother who goes away and has to be shared with other people. Thus Helen, a 6-month-old baby, who had had a very intimate and happy relationship to the breast, turned away angrily from her mother when she was being weaned and constantly wanted to go to bed where she would lie cuddling her teddy. Helen's mother felt rather rejected and hurt by Helen's preference for the teddy and this added to her own sadness at the breast-feeding having come to an end. In this situation she did not feel strong enough to battle with Helen, face her temper tantrums and tears, and so she gave in to her. Such substitutes can be convenient for both parties as they avoid painful confrontation. Yet if parents collude in the long run with such an escape from inevitable frustration and depression, they do not promote the development of close human relationships and thinking based on emotional experience. It is only the experience of someone strong enough and caring enough to tolerate painful emotional states which helps the child to feel that they can be lived through, survived and held in mind.

The child will learn on the basis of repeated experiences with those who care for him, whether his fears are capable of being borne or not, his aggression and demands set limits to or not, whether his despair and sadness can be bounded by courage and concern or have to be evaded. On the basis of containing experiences the child may take into his mind this holding capacity of his parents. This forms the basis of his internal equipment which helps him to bear emotional pain and struggle with difficulties. It is this internalised good holding mother and father which provides the internal supportive system which enables him to grow emotionally and mentally and make him less dependent on external help. At the same time, it evokes trust in the availability of reliable and helpful persons in the outside world who might be used to help him in times of need. His internal world will consequently become enriched by the example of adults who show courage in the face of adversity. All these teachers become mentors in his internal world who support him in facing difficult situations.

So far we have discussed the parental function in helping the infant to develop, but of course the baby's disposition plays just as important a part in this. Infants vary greatly from the very start in their outgoingness towards life, their capacity for receiving and responding to love. Some are hard to satisfy and continue to be unable to stand the slightest frustration without getting upset, take longer to be comforted and are easily dissatisfied. Thus each individual's experience of the nurturing received is bound to have a strong subjective component to it. There are wide variations in the way individuals make use of their experiences. Some infants are so difficult that no nurturing seems good enough: they remain fearful, suspicious and unhappy. They may e.g. experience the feeding breast, in terms of their own biting greedy feelings, as an object that will devour them. This will, of course, later become a great hindrance in learning. Others seem to make the most of even a little love and care. The more difficult the infant the harder it will be for his parents to remain patient and tolerant. Whether a mother and father are able to deal understandingly with a terrified, screaming baby, which they are bound to have to do at some time, but in some cases more than others, whether later on they are able to cope with the child's depression at weaning, whether they are able to put some limits to his greed and distinguish between anxiety and manipulation, whether they can recognise and deal with his jealousy of the parents' relationship to each other and to the next baby, will depend on what they have been able to learn on the basis of their own experience of having been infants, children, and being parented – in other words on the internal equipment which they bring to the situation. Because of the re-awakening of her own infant-self and her uncertainty about being able to cope, a mother is at first particularly vulnerable. The husband's ability to mother the mother and his belief in her capacity of being and becoming a good mother to the baby are therefore of extreme importance. Other new mothers are able to get the support of their own mother or mother-in-law; it will, of course, depend on their relationship and the rivalry that exists between them, whether this becomes a helpful or an interfering and undermining experience. Where the mother has neither external support nor a strong enough internal equipment, she will find it hard to withstand the extreme anxiety aroused by a young infant. She may wish to run away from him or become very intolerant of him whenever she feels overwhelmed. This leads to what has been called the cycle of deprivation, i.e. the tendency for deprived mothers to become depriving mothers. It is no use blaming such parents – what they need is support for their own infantile, frightened selves, re-awakened in them by their offspring.

Both partners in a relationship constantly affect each other. Thus a very responsive baby may help a mother to be less depressed and call forth her ability to care. The mother's gentle attentiveness may make the baby smile and gratify the mother and thus the couple may come ever closer together. A difficult screaming baby may overtax a mother's tolerance and her rough handling may add to the infant's panic; his screams in turn may make her less able to handle him with confidence and love, and thus a vicious circle is set up. We could say that they become increasingly maladjusted rather than learning to adjust to one another. There would thus seem to be two interwoven emotional factors involved in the capacity to learn. One is the balance of love and hate (in part an inborn factor) which colours the perception of the external world and hence what we take in and learn from experiences. The other is the extent to which parents and other important people in the child's world provide an experience of pain being modulated and thus enable the child to take in a helpful link which makes him hopeful and brave enough to explore the world and taste it fully. The child who comes to school has a wealth of experiences behind him which colour his relationship to learning and the staff. Yet school also provides him with a new opportunity to test his expectations against the reality of adults different from his parents. If he is lucky he will meet teachers who offer care, love and thoughtfulness, knowing that to be a learner involves being uncertain, frightened, angry, despairing and at times needing the assistance of others to deal with the impact of powerful emotions and anxieties.

Infantile roots of learning difficulties

In the ordinary classroom situation teachers are not usually exposed to the naked expression of anxiety. They are more likely to encounter behaviour that is the result of attempting to either keep anxiety at bay, such as lack of comprehension, inability to concentrate, confusion, or to get rid of anxiety, such as hyper-activity, fidgeting, outbursts of anger. This may have to do with some current upset in the student's relationships at school or at home. On the other hand, they may be quite specifically related to the subject matter under discussion. Because everything we experience evokes unconscious phantasies, every topic discussed at school stirs up images in the depths of the mind. If these are powerfully present and of a disturbing nature, they will temporarily or permanently interfere with learning. Taking mathematics as an example: if additions, multiplications, divisions are actually experienced by the infantile part of the child as the parents adding to the family, coming together to multiply and have babies, or as dividing and separating the members of the family (or parts of the body), it will make it hard if impossible to do sums. I remember one little girl of 10 who insisted that every sum must come to no more than one or at most two. We discovered that the reason for this was that number one stood for herself who had always to be number one, the most important person around whom the world was to revolve. She also wanted to be at one with her mother, and only grudgingly allowed the two of them to exist as separate persons. No number three, no third person, neither daddy nor another child was allowed to disturb this very close relationship, and so no sum had to exceed a total of two. The content of any lesson may reverberate with some conscious or unconscious problem in the pupil's mind. Playing with the ideas within the safety of the classroom may be a very helpful way of working them over. For instance, literature can provide the basis of coming to grips with painful human relationships. Some topics like volcanoes frequently arouse great excitement and considerable anxiety because they are closely associated with phantasies about body cavities and their dangerous contents. The science teacher may believe that nothing could be more objective than the experiments which he demonstrates and asks his pupils to perform. Yet mixing, making gases, cutting up is bound to set off all kinds of primitive phantasies. Such phantasies are universal; it is only the strength and the concreteness with which subject matter and phantasies are bound up with one another which vary. When the symbols on the page or playing with them in one's mind are equated with the enactment of a phantasy then a real block in the learning capacity of a student may occur.

The very processes involved in learning are closely analogous to that of the digestive system: taking in, digesting, absorbing, producing. The infant at first probably does not distinguish bodily processes from mental ones. He takes in food and love conjointly, experiencing pleasurable feelings when he is satisfactorily nourished. While later on mental and physical experiences come to be differentiated to some extent, the nature of the link between baby and mother forms the basis for all later experiences of taking in, retaining and giving back, whether on a mental, emotional or physical level.

Disturbances in taking in knowledge

The baby who has enjoyed being fed is likely to remain eager and trusting to open his mind to new relationships and new knowledge. When his appetite and curiosity are stimulated this leads at first to the exploration of his mother's body and later of an ever widening world. For a child who has had unreliable or depriving parenting, the feelings of helplessness aroused by not knowing may be intolerable – hence he is not open to learning but puts himself into the position of believing that he knows it all already and has no need of others. If anger and pain have dominated the earliest feeding relationship, taking in may come to be linked to fear, distrust, resentment or mere absence of an appetite for and pleasure in learning. Equally, the world may be too dangerous to explore and curiosity inhibited when this is linked in the child's mind to destructive phantasies of attacking and being attacked, conquering and being over-powered, and appropriating or being intruded upon.

Here is an example: Miss A, a first-year student at college, came to see me for a consultation, after her GP had been unable to find any physical reason for her intermittent bouts of diarrhoea and vomiting. She was a bright-looking girl with a healthy complexion, dressed in student fashion. She marched in swinging her bottom and sat down opposite me, looking rather defiant. When I asked her to tell me about her problem, she was reluctant to do so. She did not seem anxious but rather grudgingly gave me some information. I learned that she felt sick when she sat in the library and that the stomach-ache and diarrhoea occurred when listening to a lecture. She was dreading going to the reading room and lecture hall because it was embarrassing to have to rush out. When I commented that she seemed to be anxious at what others would think, she interrupted me to say – 'Not anxious, I am merely worried.' When I said that perhaps she was worried about how her behaviour might be interpreted by fellow students, she replied, with some contempt, 'Not worried – anxious.' As our conversation continued, it became clear that the continuous corrections were in no way helping to clarify the meaning, Miss A seemed rather to be simply picking on what I said. Gradually I began to stumble over words, and became almost unable to speak in coherent sentences. While finding this extremely perturbing, it occurred to me, upon reflection, that something was happening that was not dissimilar to the symptoms that Miss A had reported: the loose stools and sickness she complained of seemed to have got right into me, so that I was producing a kind of verbal diarrhoea. I put it to Miss A that she seemed to be attacking my words and to have lost sight of the fact that we were engaged in a co-operative venture of trying to understand her problem. 'Co-operative,' she exclaimed, 'I don't think of a relationship in that way at all. I always see one person as being on top and the other at the bottom.'

Now we could begin to understand something of the nature of her relationship to teachers in the lecture hall and books in the library. Those who had knowledge were experienced as being on top of her, in a superior position, forcing her to feel inferior and to be merely a bottom. The person who had something to offer was thought to use the situation in order to humiliate her. This aroused tremendous resentment and made her attack and turn into rubbish what they gave her. It would appear that coming to university, the seat of learning, revived primitive feelings in Miss A which had not been resolved in the earliest relationship to her mother, the first person who was the top person, the one with the top/breast/mind. Every relationship, far from being seen as beneficial to both partners, was felt to be one of top and bottom, superior-inferior. This, we found, affected not only her studies but her sexual experience. Such infantile feelings can arise from envy, but may also be provoked by a withholding, vain mother or teacher. When envy predominates it leads to a desire to spoil what the other person possesses. Miss A attacked me because she felt I had the ability to understand and help her. In the same way she attacked what was offered by her lecturers and the authors of the books she read because it made her feel small in comparison. Such attacks may show themselves in a much more subtle way, for instance, by always finding something to criticise about the person who is secretly admired. It is also at the root of acts of vandalism and all kinds of spoiling attacks on the creativity or beauty of others.

One way of avoiding envy is to actually experience oneself to be the person who has the desired assets by projecting oneself into him. Such a student may present as very keen to learn when, in fact, what is likely to be got hold of is no more than the external trimmings of knowledge rather than its essence. Sometimes the source of knowledge is denied and learning is obtained by stealing. Such is the case with the student who produces an essay by taking bits and pieces out of a number of books, puts them together and presents it all as his own work. Then there are children who have not been able to bear the frustration at being kept waiting for their feeds, or have had to wait too long or been given only brief spans of attention. They may not allow themselves to be taught and approach knowledge in such a greedy way that it becomes indigestible. Thus Henry, a child of 12, whose mother had little time for him, could hardly bear to listen to his teacher and constantly put up his hand, saying he knew the answer already. He had a lot of books and encyclopedias at home and seemed to swallow up their content wholesale. A great deal of attention and patience had to be shown by the teacher over a long period to allow Henry to be sure that there was enough space and time for him to take in knowledge in a less frantic manner. And then there are those children who simply turn their heads away (just like a baby when offered the spoon) apparently totally uninterested, but in fact rejecting the mental food held out to them. Their experiences may have been such that they suspect anything coming from the outside world of being dangerous or disappointing.

Difficulties in digesting and retaining knowledge

'He has a memory like a sieve,' 'in one ear and out of the other,' 'everything goes right through him,' are ways of describing individuals who seem to lack the capacity to retain an experience.

Example A

Michael has been unable to profit from ordinary classroom teaching. He sits staring out of the window sucking his pen or fingering the buttons on his jacket. He is retarded yet his eager response and ability to follow when fully held by the teacher's attention indicate that he is not unintelligent. Learning seems to be on the basis of repeating and copying what he is shown rather than thinking and developing any ideas. His teacher finds him a lovable child and his parents are attached to him. Upon enquiry, the teacher learned that Michael was an easy baby, but that his mother had been preoccupied throughout his infancy with the care of a sickly older child. Even when the mother was free to attend to him, she was emotionally unavailable. This meant that he had a mother with no space for him, one who simply presented a flat surface contact, excluding him from her mental life. Such an experience leads to a feeling that there is nowhere and no way in which thoughts and fears can be safely held. Finding no space in mother's mind, such a child does not develop a feeling of a space inside her or inside himself. Such children are often undemanding and easily drop out of the teacher's mind. It may also be more convenient for the teacher to let a child go on with his self-absorbed activities rather than yield to the great neediness for attention which he requires. A child like Michael may improve in a small group situation or remedial class where he has a place in the teacher's mind, is held and remembered there. When such children's hope in someone able to bear their distress is re-awakened they often become very possessive and powerful emotions come to the fore. If the child then becomes more demanding and sometimes shows violent feelings the teacher may think that he has become worse, when actually he is a bit better at protesting and making his needs known. On the basis of very special attention given to such children, they are sometimes able to make astonishing progress. Others are so flat and withdrawn that any amount of attention is insufficient. Yet others who seem less obviously disturbed seem to acquire knowledge on the basis of imitation and learning by rote. They may even appear clever and intellectual but their ideas are lacking in depth and richness.

We all have a tendency to become mindless at times when our experiences become too painful to think about. We may simply switch off or alternatively drown our sorrow in drink, drug it with loud noise and bright lights, or escape into non-stop activity. Mental pain that cannot be thought about may be experienced as a somatic disturbance, as in the following example.

Example B

Jill was a 14-year-old girl suffering from debilitating migraines, which necessitated repeated absences from school, sometimes for weeks on end. She was eventually referred to a Child Guidance Clinic and when asked by her therapist about the onset of her headaches, Jill was quite sure that they had started on the day that the cafeteria staff were undermanned. The whole system seemed to go out of order and the children who had to stand in a line for a long time waiting, became rough and noisy. This Jill had found difficult to bear. Later on she had repeatedly tried to work out the cost of different items on the menu – she knew the overall price but insisted that she wanted to know the different amounts which made up the total sum. She was polite to her therapist, concerned that she shouldn't be overworked, and visualised hundreds of children crowding into her room making demands on her. She spoke in such a flat tone of voice, without any show of emotion, that it was difficult for the therapist to sense what the girl was feeling. Gradually she came to appreciate that the incident in the cafetaria had been so disturbing to Jill, because it corresponded so closely to her experience of her mother. Jill's mother had married very young and, after many rows and the births of several children, the husband had eventually left her. Mother felt lonely, unable to cope without the support of her husband, and when she feels overwhelmed, spills out her worries to the children. Jill's obsession with working out the different items on the menu might be seen as an attempt to isolate the different parts of her experience of her mother, making sense of what she gets from her rather than accepting an indigestible meal. It emerged that Jill's headaches occurred whenever she felt she had too much to do, or that the work was of too great a complexity. She tried to deal with her headaches sometimes by rolling her head backwards, as she said, 'to make more space there' for the pain. Her headaches appear thus to be the result of having taken in a mother who has not enough space for, nor the strength to help bear the emotional pain. Jill has always been aware that her mother was not unkind or unwilling but simply overwhelmed by the demands made on her. Jill attempted to spare her mother, to try to keep her difficulties to herself, yet could not manage this situation. Unlike the student Miss A, Jill responded eagerly and gratefully to the opportunity to being listened to and understood. Her headaches soon cleared up and she was able to return to school on a regular basis. She is unlikely to have ever asked for special help as she had no experience and little hope of anyone being willing and able to hold her emotionality. It was only when her mental pain became a physical symptom that the need for some intervention became apparent to everyone. It is interesting to note that once her therapist was experienced as a stronger personality than her mother who could contain anxieties, the more destructive parts of Jill's personality were brought for attention.

Problems related to producing work

Producing work faces us with the anxiety about what we contain. Are we empty? Are we full of mess? By what means have we acquired what we do possess? What have we done to what has been given to us: have we destroyed it or lost it ? Will we be able to sort out our thoughts, formulate out of chaos and confusion something that is communicable to others? Some degree of anxiety is an inevitable concomitant of engaging in creative work. Some individuals, however, find themselves crippled in such situations. Performing and sitting for examinations inevitably evoke anxieties about being judged and found to be wrong or inadequate. Examinations may be experienced as a screening which enables the examiner to see right inside and discover all the shameful and forbidden aspects of the personality. The examiner may be thought to be a harsh judge demanding unrealistic standards, or he may be an envious parent wishing to keep the student from entering upon the next stage of adulthood. Feelings of competition with peers and adults further add to making any test a fraught experience. The atmosphere in schools and colleges during 'Finals' is often one of fear, fierce rivalry and despair – 'every man for himself'.

Example A: Despair and depression

'I can't do it, I haven't anything to say, I simply can't,' 15-year-old John exclaimed whenever he was asked to do his homework. He would evade it by playing with his friends, coming home late, and although he was labelled 'lazy' at first, it later became evident that he felt hopeless and despairing. His teacher was concerned that this youngster should be able to sit for his examinations, yet the way that John had given up trying to work seemed to make the prospect of his passing a test quite unrealistic. When he talked to John about the future, the boy appeared to have no aspirations. He described his father as extremely successful and John could not imagine ever emulating him. It gradually emerged that John regarded the examination as a final test of manhood, and that he would be expected to take his place among the adults as a fully mature person once he had passed. No wonder, seeing exams in that light, made John frightened that his mental and sexual potency were inadequate for such a task! Talks with his teacher enabled John to realise that he had a long way to go before he would be expected to take up fully adult responsibility. This and an encouragement to produce short essays instead of aiming at 'works of art' gradually relieved John's anxiety and made him able to face examinations with less feelings of despair.

Example B: Rivalry and triumph

Mr C is a talented flautist who showed promise early in life. Both his parents were musical but did not have the opportunity to fully develop their gifts. Mr C became the centre of his parents' attention, their pride and joy. He was an excellent student of music but became terrified before every performance. Once on stage he did very well, became excited by his success, but subsequently experienced feelings of emptiness and depression. Talking about it revealed that to perform was felt to make an exhibition of himself and show himself to be more successful than his parents. He felt no indebtedness to them for the talent he had inherited nor for the sacrifices they had brought on his behalf in order to give him a good musical education. On the contrary, he despised his parents, their working-class accent and rough manners. Nor was his relationship to music one of love and devotion; rather he experienced himself to be the creator and embodiment of the music he performed. Although he considered himself to be outstandingly gifted he was plagued by a constant fear of failure. He imagined that his listeners were out to find fault, to show him up as being, after all, imperfect. In other words they were experienced as wanting to triumph over him in the same way as he felt he had triumphed over his parents. His success was felt to be at other people's expense and hence they were thought to be depleted and deeply resentful.

In this chapter I have mentioned but a few examples of difficulties related to learning, thinking and using knowledge and skills. More detailed descriptions of learning difficulties and the function of the teacher as a container of anxieties and facilitator of thinking, will be given in Part III.

Part III

Understanding the individual child in the classroom

G. Henry

Chapter 5

Idealised relationships

In this, and the subsequent two chapers, we shall look at examples which teachers brought from their work experience. Many instances of idealisation were brought by teachers to our work discussion group. The problem of idealisation is so complex and has so many facets that it might be helpful to focus on one of them at a time. In some cases, the idealisation of the teacher-counsellor was particularly evident. In others, a child or young adult was exerting great pressure to *be* idealised by the teacher. Those two aspects are usually closely related, but I have tried to select examples where one or the other predominates.

Unreasonable demands on the teacher

It may be difficult to continue perceiving oneself as a useful and helpful person when the demands made are very excessive and out of proportion with what one could possibly offer. The pressure to overstep one's limits and to go 'out of one's way to be helpful' can in those cases be very strong.

One such example was presented by a teacher in Further Education. She was extremely worried about the extent of her commitment and responsibility for one of her students. Mrs V prefaced her presentation by saying that she felt she had got very involved, perhaps over-involved with Sandy. This student of 22 years left school with no qualifications and had recently enrolled at college. She lived in a hostel and had no contact with her family. Mrs V had occasionally been meeting her after lessons, and at student gatherings at the pub. The first incident which caused Mrs V alarm occurred one day when she was leaving the college and Sandy, looking very dreamy and lost, informed her that she had taken an 'LSD trip', and was still under the drug's influence and frightened. Mrs V felt very alarmed, but was not sure that Sandy was so afraid herself as she seemed so 'switched off'. Sandy related that she had taken what she knew to be a dangerous amount. Mrs V took her home and Sandy stayed at the teacher's flat for the night and recovered. There were two more such episodes when the girl came to stay at Mrs V's flat.

When students were informed that they could choose a personal tutor amongst the teachers at college, Sandy decided on Mrs V who felt she had no option and could not refuse. She told our group that her attempt to establish a more conventional tutor/tutee relationship with Sandy remained unsuccessful. All suggestions to meet at pre-arranged times, and for definite lengths of time, were met by a wall of silence. It was clear, Mrs V said, that Sandy's demands were limitless. On one particular occasion, Sandy telephoned her saying that she had taken 'a lot of drugs', and asked Mrs V to come to her flat. The teacher went, but Sandy was in too doped a state to talk. Mrs V felt overwhelmed by panic. She tried to take the girl to hospital but Sandy refused to go. So Mrs V 'phoned an ambulance. Again Sandy objected: 'I am staying here and you are to look after me.' She did not appear worried in the least. Finally, the police were sent for and Sandy was admitted to hospital. She was to stay there for at least a day, but discharged herself. Mrs V met her on the street and escorted her back to hospital.

Giving a very vivid account of this dramatic occurrence, Mrs V told us that she had been 'frightened to death' by the responsibility she had taken on. She had been put in the position of being responsible for Sandy's life. If she backed out of the role Sandy put her in, she was sure Sandy would die. Sandy had rejected the appropriate agencies, the doctor, the ambulance men, the hospital staff. The demands on Mrs V were unrealistic, yet she felt she had to fulfil Sandy's expectations. She told us that a strictly tutor/tutee relationship would be so inadequate to Sandy's needs, that it wasn't worth offering, it felt too incongruous: 'It would be like sending a packet of tea to relieve the famine in Ethiopia.' The discussion about this example brought us to understand that Sandy was actually making Mrs V feel that she had to be a mother who devoted herself entirely to her young baby, a mother who should be there always, or else the baby might die. In fact a mother who would take completely on herself the worry and the anxiety whether the baby stayed alive. One would not expect a baby to look after himself nor did Sandy worry once Mrs V arrived. Mrs V was burdened with the worry. She panicked and felt 'frightened to death', carrying in fact the fear of death that Sandy was not experiencing herself. Just like a baby may well not accept care from anyone but his mother, Sandy clearly spelled out – 'I am staying here and you are to look after me.' Obviously she was being unrealistic, but idealisation *is* out of touch with reality and it is a very early and primitive way of relating.

Mrs V was aware that she had to set a limit at some stage to Sandy's unlimited demands; she had in fact suggested that she see a doctor, but had only met with a negative response. Sandy told Mrs V that she had already 'beaten two psychiatrists by not saying a word during the interviews'. Mrs V felt particularly worried when Sandy told her that she should soon leave her hostel, and asked whether she could stay at Mrs V's flat until she found an alternative accommodation. She thought she could not possibly accept this intrusion into her family life, yet where was Sandy to go? Fortunately, the hostel decided she could stay on until some alternative accommodation could be found.

Mrs V said she found it most difficult to set limits because of the possible consequences, chiefly the threat of suicide. The group discussed whether Mrs V's involvement was in fact helpful to Sandy. After all, a point would come when limits would have to be set and this would be all the harder for Sandy to accept the longer it was delayed. It would not only disappoint her, but it was probably going to cause a great deal of rage; Mrs V had better be ready for this reaction if she were to try and change her relationship to Sandy. Was she perhaps afraid that, having been put on a pedestal, she might now be thrown into a very denigrated role if she were to say: 'I cannot give you all you want from me.' Falling from a pedestal can certainly cause more bruises than falling from ground level. Although Sandy might well consider whatever was offered instead to be worthless, the crucial problem was whether Mrs V had been drawn so much into an idealised relationship that *she* had come to agree that all else *was* worthless. In a way she appeared to do so when she referred to the 'packet of tea sent to starving Ethiopia'.

One of Sandy's problems appeared to be a great deal of confusion. Indeed this had a very strong impact not only on Mrs V, but on our group. It was as if Sandy's perceptions imposed themselves very forcefully even at a distance. After some hard work we seemed to agree that Sandy badly needed to be helped to sort out what belonged where, and who could do what. Although she might kick against the setting of limits, it would be a very valuable experience for her. She was often in a daze which resulted in blurring the boundaries for herself and others. For a while I sensed that our group perceived that now we were somehow responsible for Sandy's life.

Some months later we again heard about Sandy. At this time we had started presenting some cases through role playing. Most members of the group found it helped them to empathise with the child or student they presented. Miss D, another member of the group, volunteered to play the tutor. Mrs V told us that Sandy now, albeit reluctantly, came to see her at a pre-arranged time.

Mrs V, acting Sandy, walked to the empty chair stamping her feet. Her nose was slightly wrinkled, a frown on her forehead. She sat leaning back in the chair stretching her legs. She didn't answer Miss D's greeting, but looked intensely at a spot on the floor. When Miss D asked, 'How are things?', she looked up with a sullen expression, saying 'OK, why do you ask?' Miss D pointed out that Sandy seemed to feel she had asked just out of politeness, not because she really wanted to know. Sandy answered rather spitefully, 'You couldn't care for all the people you have got on your books, could you, you have got to get on with your job – how are things Sandy, and who is next?' Miss D said Sandy knew she had thirty minutes of her time, it was not going to be 'how are things and who is next?', but thirty minutes seemed to be felt by Sandy as a very short amount of time. As the interview progressed, there was some communication over problems of accommodation. Sandy had found digs but was not too pleased with them. Suddenly Sandy volunteered the information that she had been made President of the Students' Union (this had actually happened); she sounded very pleased about it. Miss D asked for some information about the work that this involved. Sandy told her and also added rather angrily that she had been to see her 'shrink', but she did not think he was much good.

Sandy eventually had accepted seeing a psychiatrist and this helped the establishment of a more manageable relationship with Mrs V. She was obviously implying all the time that were Mrs V prepared to take her back 'on her lap again', she would turn her back on the daddy-shrink at a moment's notice. One of the points we discussed later was how easily one is tempted by this type of seduction. Miss D said she had to resist her wish to ask in which way the psychiatrist was no good. She realised that it would have been taken by Sandy as an invitation to flatter her and tell her how much better she was. We also looked at the feeling conveyed by the word 'shrink' in the context of the growing pains Sandy appeared to be experiencing and was kicking against. Indeed the quality of her relationships appeared to be shrinking from a fairy tale dimension to a more human one. She still appeared to imply on the one hand that tutors with so many people on their books, mothers who can't give their undivided attention to one child are no good, don't care; yet, on the other hand, she seemed to be gradually coming to terms in a sullen way with making use of what could be offered. She had not turned her back on the tutor altogether as Mrs V had feared she would; nor had she killed herself. In fact there had been no more very dramatic incidents in her relationship with Mrs V; she had even agreed to come and see her at a given time. This process of the 'shrinking' of one's expectation is a painful one and Sandy certainly found it so. Her need to be hurtful could perhaps partly be understood as a way of disposing of some of her pain, getting someone else to feel it. ('Why do you ask?' was a good example of this – Miss D said it made her feel she was being punched in the stomach.) Her rage was against the 'shrinker' of her expectations and this applied to Mrs V too, not only to the psychiatrist.

Idealisation of teacher and self

Mrs L presented a very detailed account of the development of her relationship with Tina, a 17-year-old girl from a Middle-Eastern country, who had recently come to England and joined the grammar school where Mrs L is teaching. When Tina first met Mrs L, who was in charge of the science department, she expressed a wish to study mathematics, chemistry, physics, zoology and English in the sixth form. She stated that she had come to this country because of the greater educational and career opportunities. She looked upon England as 'her Mecca'. The very high score Tina obtained in a multiple-choice test showed that her previous education had been of a high standard. In spite of Tina's unquestionable eagerness and good intelligence, Mrs L gained the impression that the girl had a strong tendency to over-exert herself. She felt she should limit Tina's expectations about the amount of work she could reasonably hope to do. Tina accepted this reluctantly. For a term Mrs L's personal contact with Tina was purely in relation to work in science subjects. However, at the beginning of the second term Tina approached Mrs L during a free period in the chemistry laboratory. Mrs L noticed that Tina looked anxious and invited her to sit down. Tina burst out: 'Do you psycho-analyse people?' (Tina was a very widely read girl and had been looking up a number of books about therapeutic help. In spite of her intelligence and sophistication, she distorted whatever she may have read about psycho-analysis into some naive notion of a magical cure.) Mrs L was rather taken aback and answered, 'No, why do you ask?' Tina replied that she needed help because she wasn't 'normal'. She went on to explain that she couldn't communicate with people, always felt an outsider. It wasn't a language problem, since even at home she could not 'laugh at a joke nor feel one of a crowd'. She had never been able to mix easily and now it was worse than ever. It emerged that Tina had only joined with others when she had been in the position to take the lead. She said she felt very disappointed about the attitude of her classmates to education, they were not like the English people she had met back home. This was not the case with Mrs L whom she 'admired very much'. In reporting this to the group, Mrs L described her response to this declaration: 'I felt taken aback and I laughed briefly in embarrassment.'

In the discussion that followed, Mrs L stressed her discomfort then as also when Tina had asked her: 'Do you psycho-analyse people?' She had similar feelings of unease when Tina began to describe one of her main problems, saying: 'There is something that I hate in myself which concerns my father.' She found it difficult to tell Mrs L, but eventually said that she so hated the 'animal noises' her father made when he ate that she couldn't eat at the same table. This was not the only idiosyncrasy which afflicted Tina, but rather than enumerating them, it might be more useful to focus on Tina's perceptions of the world in terms of wonderful and dreadful and the impact this had on Mrs L. Mrs L felt at the end of this meeting – 'I didn't want Tina to think that although I could not offer her a solution right away, she had come in vain or was being abandoned to her despair.' Mrs L thought she should leave Tina something good to hang on to until they met again and recommended a book to read, and in particular an essay entitled 'Valueing the Self'.

When they met after the weekend Tina told her that she had read most of the essays in the book and found them very interesting, especially the one entitled 'Doubt and Indecision'. 'Doubt and Indecision' was indeed what had been strongly aroused in Mrs L herself in the first encounter with Tina. She was taken aback by Tina's rather abrupt request to be psycho-analysed and given an immediate solution to her problems. She felt over-whelmed by the girl's obviously great expectations of her as a helper and very unsure as to how she could live up to them. We began to discuss in our group whether Tina really experienced admiration for Mrs L or was it not rather some tremendous expectation she put upon her? The world appeared to be divided for Tina into two neat, intensely separate halves. On the one hand England, culture, the Mecca and Mrs L were merged into a greatly idealised cluster, while, on the other lay the despised home country, all Englishmen not up to 'Mecca' standards and, worst of all, her 'subhuman' father. (It is significant that Tina's level of education when she came to England was so very high, proving that her own capacity to assess what her own country had given her was severely impaired by her despising attitude towards it.)

Mrs L's discomfort at being so 'admired' was perhaps understandable: she wasn't being admired, she was idealised. She was supposed to respond to the expectations of a totally providing, almost holy object (the Mecca) who could solve problems (psycho-analysis being seen as a miracle cure). To a certain extent, Mrs L felt compelled to respond to this pressure to be ideal when she experienced guilt at letting Tina go away 'empty-handed'. This led to providing her with weekend reading about 'valueing the self'. Mrs L told us that her doubts about her capacity to help Tina made her feel that she herself needed to read something about 'valueing the self'. Being idealised triggers off enormous fears about one's actual value. If one in the least falls for it or colludes with it, one knows that the alternatives are unequivocal: either one has to be an unfailing person, a sort of oracle dispensing answers and miracle cures, or one is useless, no good at all, experienced as rubbish. Perhaps one of Mrs L's most helpful remarks in her conversation with Tina was when she spoke about the impossibly high standards we sometimes set ourselves and others; then when we fail to live up to them we feel that we are considered by others, but most of all by ourselves, to be no good at all.

A while after this talk Tina decided that she had taken on more work than she could cope with and decided to drop her study of physics. She appeared very relieved and more cheerful. One day, though, Tina again came looking very distraught, exclaiming: 'When will it end? I feel as though I want to go to sleep to escape from the misery for a time.' She did not reveal what the misery was about. Mrs L was dismayed, worried that perhaps she had taken on greater responsibility for this girl than she could cope with. She thought that Tina ought really to see a doctor if her difficulties were as serious as all that. She discussed this with Tina who promised to get in touch with her GP. It appeared, subsequently, that the very fact that Mrs L had felt so hopeless, worried and recognised her own limitations had helped Tina greatly. She told Mrs L some days later: 'It was as if someone had lifted a weight off my shoulders,' and she overcame this bad patch without needing to seek medical advice. The very fact that Mrs L could say, 'Sorry, but you are asking me for the sort of help I am unable to give you,' without losing her belief that something valuable could be preserved in her relationship with her student, might have opened a new possibility for Tina. It might have given her a glimpse of a world where people need not feel either extraordinarily clever or totally hopeless. This alternative can be felt perhaps as much less attractive because it is fraught with a great deal of 'doubt and indecision', and the continuous reassessment of one's judgments and one's capacities.

A fairy-tale world in black and white (witches and fairy-godmothers) exposes one to dramatic fluctuations, but it frees one from conflict, guilt and uncertainty. The price to be paid is high as human relationships are cast into a totally unrealistic mould, but people, countries, all of one's life experiences can be fitted into one of two neat slots. The filing system is greatly simplified.

Attempts at polarisation

It is interesting that in the cases of both Sandy and Tina there were attempts to establish an idealised relationship with a mother-figure while trying to keep the father-figure relegated to a secondary or denigrated role. Tina's father was indeed as much denigrated as Mrs L was idealised. In the material Mrs V presented, we saw how Sandy, in planning to take over the living room of Mrs V's flat, pretended Mr V did not exist. She was also openly denigratory of the male psychiatrist. In this context we can see that Miss D was being very helpful to Sandy when she resisted the temptation to elicit grievances against the 'shrink'. She behaved like a parent who will not allow herself to be idealised at the expense of the other partner. She could so easily have channelled the rage and the contempt towards the psychiatrist and thus have spared herself Sandy's tantrums. Sandy might have felt more comfortable if she had been allowed to experience all her negative feelings towards the 'nasty daddy' and blissfully cuddled up to 'mummy' again. So often when trying to help children with their problems one has to choose between the temporarily easy way out and helping them face inevitable frustrations. Growth just doesn't seem to come about if one's main aim is to preserve a comfortable situation for oneself and them.

The type of wedging that was rather striking in the previous examples, as an attempt to set 'mummy' against 'daddy', appears to present itself in countless and often less obvious ways in the school situation. Miss F is an English teacher. She told us of 12-year-old Sharon, who said she only attended school because of English Literature. All other lessons were boring, all other teachers hopeless. Later that evening the same teacher told us of her difficulties with Kevin. He constantly doodled in her lessons, never paid any attention to what she said, produced only a few lines when asked to write an essay. He absolutely worshipped the maths teacher and worked very hard for him. Even allowing for a difference of interests and attitudes, we felt that the main task of our group was to explore the quality of the relationships described by Miss F. During the discussion she told us that she had asked the maths teacher to use his influence on Kevin to see if he could persuade the boy to give a little more of his very good mind to other subjects than maths. In a way it seemed she had asked the teacher to be a little generous towards his colleagues. Kevin's idealisation of his favourite subject and teacher was costing them all too much. This led Miss F to ask herself how far she might have encouraged and could discourage Sharon's idealisation of English Literature and herself, and wondered if her colleagues resented her to the same extent that she had resented the maths teacher's special relationship with Kevin. She was very receptive in her observation of how different it feels to be at the receiving end of the idealisation or to be paying the price of being the opposite – the 'bad, boring one'. A member of the group suggested that teachers should protect one another from the ill-effects of what he called 'the wedge game'. He could think of a few examples in his school where relationships amongst colleagues had been profoundly undermined, especially when one member of the staff had become a sort of idol for many of the children and appeared to enjoy this role. Perhaps, the group member added, his colleague did not realise that others were paying the bill for his being idolised.

We discussed a similar problem in a different context when a teacher in Further Education, Mr W, told us of the very disconcerting experience he had had with one of his tutees. The first time he saw Colin, a young man in his late twenties, he presented him with an incredible variety of problems ranging from grant, accommodation, curriculum to very serious personal difficulties. He felt he was expected to be a miracle worker who had to offer instant solutions for all these problems. His feeling was probably akin to the one experienced by Mrs L when Tina approached her and asked her abruptly 'Do you psycho-analyse people?' When the tutor told Colin that all those difficulties could not be sorted out immediately and they should meet again to try and deal with them little by little, Colin got up, left the room in a huff and did not return to the tutor for nearly a month.

This last instance shows that Mrs V's anxieties that Sandy might have turned her back on her were not altogether unfounded. If one does not accept idealisation and the unlimited demands that go with it, one does in fact run that risk. Mr W told us that during the time when Colin had avoided his tutor, he had apparently 'done the rounds' of other members of staff, in an attempt to find someone else prepared to work miracles. Fortunately there appeared to be a 'mutual agreement' amongst the staff members as Colin did not find someone willing to compete with his tutor and to collude with his 'wedge game'. But one could imagine that had Colin found an ally while doing his rounds, Mr W's attempts to curb his unrealistic expectations would have been sabotaged. This problem might arise especially in large schools or institutions because of the difficulty of communication which can make it only too easy for a student to play the 'wedge game' with great success and often set members of staff against one another.

Idealisation and denigration

'You're not like my Mum'

It is not infrequent for this type of situation to arise in the relationship between home and school. Some children may bring such a convincing picture of gloom and speak of their parents in such a derogatory way, that their version is accepted without reservation. The child is pitied and the teacher feels that he or she has to compensate with her relationship for the difficulties experienced at home. It is very difficult not to be flattered by a child who tells you: 'You're nice Miss; you never shout. You're not like my mum.'

An interesting example of this was brought by a teacher in one of our groups. She told us about Annette, a 12-year-old, who had said at the end of her cookery lesson that it was not worth taking her biscuits home as her mother would say that they were rubbish and would throw them in the dustbin. The teacher had no opportunity to meet Annette's mother until an Open Day some while later and had until then kept in her mind the image of an insensitive and rejecting person. She was very surprised when she met someone whom she perceived to be genuinely warm and concerned for her child. It occurred to us that Annette's comment about something being thrown in the dustbin was indeed very meaningful and that it was important not to collude with her attempts to denigrate her mother in the eyes of the teacher and treat her like rubbish.

It may happen at times that what children say about their home life is quite accurate; they may have a very difficult situation to contend with and a teacher may have reason to sympathise with the child in this respect, just as one may on occasion share a child's reservations about another member of staff. Given this situation one has to take into account what attitude is most helpful *to the child*. There is a very considerable difference between being prepared to listen to difficulties and encouraging grievances. We have up to now been looking mainly at *one* particular aspect of the 'wedge game', i.e. its consequences in creating a rift between colleagues or between school and home, but it is important to remember that this is paralleled by the child wedging apart his or her feelings and that there is, in many children, a strong tendency to do this even without any external support. Growing pains are by-passed by clinging to a fairy-tale picture of the world, where one can meet only witches or fairy-godmothers and where the painful experience of having mixed feelings for one and the same person is avoided. Sandy offered us a very good example of how she found it difficult to relinquish this attitude, and we have also seen that she needed as much help as she could get, to struggle against it in order to grow up. The wedge *within her* profoundly interfered with her development.

Comfort or development

I mentioned earlier the choice between 'comfort or development' as the frequent alternative one is confronted with, and we saw how it appeared very unlikely that Tina or Sandy, for instance, could 'have it easy' and grow up at the same time. It may be useful to take a second look at the type of 'comfort' they were looking for and examine whether that state of affairs was really so comfortable. Tina had certainly reservations about 'being one of a crowd'. She said she had only mixed with others when she had been in the position to take the lead and there was little doubt that she wished to be 'treated as special' in the relationship with Mrs L. She put across the feeling that she was too good for the standards of her home country, so she didn't belong there and she appeared to feel too good for her peer group in England as well. Had Mrs L accepted her bid for mutual idealisation, 'doubt and indecision' would perhaps have been by-passed, but Tina's feeling of isolation would probably have been reinforced. The 'teacher's pet' is never a very popular character and is very often, in the depths, a very frightened child, always on guard in case the other children whom he has made jealous and envious may overthrow him from his privileged position. Furthermore, we saw that there are no half ways in the black and white dimension; from being very special one might risk ending up on the rubbish heap. Adolescents often have their anxieties reinforced in this respect by looking at the fate of the precarious idols in the pop music world. Top of the charts one month, forgotten the next; the speed of their rise and fall can be very alarming and disconcerting.

If we look at the frightened child in Sandy, we can see how her expectation to be protected by an all-giving, always present, idealised mother who would take total responsibility for her, was probably borne out by a wish to have someone carry all her fears for her; it was as if she said: 'I can't dream my nightmare, I need someone very strong to do it for me,' but it is doubtful that her fears were diminished in depth at the time when Mrs V colluded with her demands. Somewhere, somehow, Sandy must have known it couldn't last and we saw that there was more to her than a 22-year-old baby, that she had good contact with reality when it came to the Students' Union. Perhaps she had become so clinging and wanted to make herself a niche right in Mrs V's flat, because she sensed that her position was precarious. Once she stopped having full-time attention, she had great doubts as to whether she could be held *at all* in Mrs V's mind, be one of the people she cared for ('you couldn't possibly care for all the people on your books'). This would point to an expectation of being totally forgotten, being 'thrown away'. The vicious circle becomes clearer if we see Sandy's demands for special protection being partly motivated by fear and anxiety, but also getting undivided attention as a potential source of fear and anxiety.

Sandy probably perceived that Mrs V was getting very close to the end of her tether. This was in fact so, for in her first presentation to the group Mrs V said that as Sandy's demands increased, it had crossed her mind to quit her job, as the only possible escape from such an untenable situation. She did not really intend to carry this out, but it was extremely helpful that she shared this thought with the group, as it gave us the measure of the anxiety that she had to deal with. She experienced her time and mind, as well as her flat, to be completely invaded. She was made to feel responsible for the life of a girl who behaved in a totally dependent way and found it very difficult indeed to tolerate this anxiety or to attempt to modify a situation that had been gradually escalating.

When we look at this aspect of the situation, we see that in spite of the apparent comfort of an initial honeymoon period, a relationship based on idealisation is very likely to evoke a number of anxieties in the long or short run, both in the child and in the teacher. It is doubtful that these are preferrable to the anxieties that are being by-passed; in fact it might turn out to be rather a 'poor exchange'.

Chapter 6

Denigratory relationships

Denigration has often been referred to in the previous chapter as the necessary counterpart of idealisation. If *all* positive feelings are lodged in one person, or a group of persons, or an idea/ideal, they become totally divorced from negative feelings. The latter will need to find a more or less willing receptacle to be black-washed (denigrate, from the Latin denigrare, meaning to blacken).

There are cases where denigration is very evident but the idealisation is somewhat less apparent. Both the girls described in the previous chapter were seeking a relationship of total and unrealistic dependency on their teachers. It may be useful, now, to consider examples where the wish for being mothered is denied, i.e. a rejection of any feeling of dependency: the 'I-don't-need-anybody' type of child. In those cases denigration looms large and idealisation, though present, can be seen in the form of *self-idealisation*.

Example 1 Intolerance of dependency

Paul is a 9-year-old boy described by his teacher, Mr D, as an 'unteachable clever child'. When the teacher attempted to help him assimilate some basic concepts of mathematics, Paul would say that he could not be bothered with maths because his only interest was space technology, or else complain that the teaching wasn't up to his own standard. Often, Mr D felt at a loss with him and at the end of his tether. We heard that Paul was very involved with a younger brother, Simon. He tended to play mother to Simon in a variety of ways and 'smother' him. Simon was a sturdy 8-year-old, who did not at all welcome his brother's over-protective attitude; he objected at being taken to the toilet or helped to unwrap his packed lunch. Mr D related that Paul looked *'pathetic'* when Simon rejected his help, but had behaved like the 'most solicitous of nurses' when Simon, on one occasion, fell in the playground and grazed his knee. He told us that he so desperately needed Simon to need him that he might have welcomed a more serious injury than a grazed knee. This very perceptive teacher appeared to be aware that this behaviour was due to something other than an overflow of brotherly love.

Paul had great difficulties in mixing with other boys in class and was not at all popular with them. He treated girls in a somewhat superior way, yet some of them appeared to find his chauvinistic kind of behaviour attractive. Paul was the only one in the class who treated an educationally subnormal girl, Mary, with ruthless contempt; for instance, he drew a picture of Mary with her head down the lavatory.

At a parents' meeting, the teacher learnt that Paul's mother was a very disheartened woman who wished 'her little boy gave her a chance to help him.' She had heard Paul cry at night more than once, but felt that, had she gone to him, he certainly would have pushed her off and would have denied that he had ever been crying. This she knew from previous experiences, but also was aware that Paul needed a helping hand and was very miserable, yet she felt her hands to be completely tied. Like Mr D, she was at a loss as to how to help him. She was also concerned about her child's learning difficulties. She said she thought he must have a good mind because he was quite an expert about anything to do with outer space.

Mr D told us that meeting Paul's mother had helped him give a name to the feeling Paul evoked in him. He could sense, although he had never seen him crying, that he was a very unhappy child, continually trying to deny his weaknesses. After this communication there was a considerable shift in the mood of the teacher's group. They had reacted at first with profound distaste to the description of Paul's drawing (the one about the emotionally subnormal girl). I suggested that, unsavoury and off-putting as that piece of behaviour might be, we could try and understand it in terms of Paul's need to disown and locate in someone else a 'sub-standard' part of himself (indeed he was not a very brilliant scholar), for which the little educationally subnormal girl became a very suitable receptacle. His drawing showed how he wished to flush down the drain this denigrated, unacceptable aspect of himself, so that he could preserve an unblemished self-idealised picture of 'Paul the space technologist.' As we were discussing the sub-standard part of Paul, Mr D reminded us that he had been told in no uncertain terms that his teaching methods were 'sub-standard'. Did Paul perhaps want him to feel a little educationally subnormal as well? The group laughed at this comment, but I questioned whether we might not be trying to find a comic aspect in Paul's behaviour, because we all found it hard to stay with its tragic quality. Here was a boy, obviously in need of help, of teaching and nurturing, most of all of being understood, but so intolerant of any feeling of dependency that he tried to ignore it and to disown it, attempting instead to mother his brother, attempting to foster better teaching standards in his teacher. Yet he was alone with his tears. His mother was not to know what the tears were about, nor were we. We could only make some hypotheses. For instance, that Paul's system of defences may not be all that water-tight (tear-proof) and that the small needy child he lodged in the unwilling Simon, and the under-achiever he lodged in the ESN girl Mary, did not in fact go down the drain; that those feelings of inadequacy confronted him in his loneliness and *with* his loneliness.

As we meet at times children much harder than Paul whose denial of dependency is almost 'water-tight', it was hopeful to know that Paul had chinks in his armour of self-idealisation. His mother was probably right in feeling that she would be perceived as trespassing, had she gone into his bedroom while he was crying. We discussed what could be most helpful in terms of Mr D's relationship with Paul. It was not a matter of breaking and entering into any chink in his armour, for instance at the times when Paul looked pathetic as his attempts to mother Simon were defeated. Mr D agreed he didn't wish to take Paul offguard and somehow confront him with his weakness when 'he looked wobbly'. He could, on the other hand, resist the temptation of bending over backwards to find attractive devices in order to seduce Paul into accepting some of the food for thought he was offering, as he had done in the past. This can be seen as the equivalent of the acrobatics some mothers of poor feeders are prepared to perform in order to entice their children into eating. Such behaviour is often the consequence of feeling so disheartened by the continual refusal of what is being offered that teachers and mothers alike may be overwhelmed by the unbearable pain of rejection, and somehow see no alternative to playing tricks or, as one of the teachers in the group put it: 'devising the right commercial in order to sell a poor product'. Mr D told us that when he had felt at the end of his tether or at a loss with Paul, he had actually, more than once, begun to doubt the quality of his teaching.

There was abundant evidence that Paul might have a very strong need to lodge his feelings of inadequacy in someone else, and that his projections (disowning and delegation) of such feelings might have been very powerful indeed. Mr D had said very sensitively that it would be a matter of 'finding the right sort of smile' when Paul confronted him again with some contemptuous assessment of his performance as a teacher. Not a sarcastic smile conveying 'stop teaching your grandmother how to suck eggs', but a smile conveying the feeling that while he understood how Paul felt, he was not in agreement with his assessment. Somebody in the group suggested that maybe a friendly jokey remark such as 'nobody's perfect' might convey the feeling that Mr D was not shattered by Paul's denigra-tion. Should this experience even slightly decrease Paul's self-idealisation, it could contribute to encourage him to descend from outer space (his interest in space technology was certainly not meaningless), and might eventually enable him to accept a helping hand. There seemed to be a hope that, given time and a number of experiences where Paul's pattern of defences were not colluded with, his trust in somebody who attempts to feed him, understand him, without making him utterly dependent, could gradually develop. We were left wondering about this because Paul had only one more year in primary school (fortunately Mr D was going to go up with him) and the transition to secondary school was very likely to present further problems.

Example 2 The gang as a protection against dependency

I would like now to describe an adolescent boy who presents in some respects a much more hardened version of Paul, with few chinks in his armour of self-idealisation.

Richard, a 15-year-old boy, was presented by Mrs T, a French teacher. She told us that she had had to be away because of illness for the first lesson after the Christmas break, and a substitute teacher – Mr S – had taken the class instead. Richard came late to the subsequent lesson. As he entered the class, he said with obvious disappointment: 'Isn't the other chap here, Miss?' When Mrs T reminded him that Mr S was a substitute teacher, Richard commented 'Oh, what a pity – he loved Genesis'; Genesis being a pop group Richard is 'almost addicted to'.

Mrs T told us that one of the girls in the class, Nadia, 'a specialist in telling tales', reported that they had done almost no work at all with Mr S – he had spent most of his time talking with Richard about Genesis. Richard had told Mr S how Mrs T would never have allowed him to talk about Genesis and added, 'I expect she is too old for pop music.' When asked by Mr S about Mrs T's age, Richard had answered: 'Oh, she is a middle-aged bird' (Mrs T is in reality a very attractive woman in her early thirties).

I will now quote from Mrs T's description which was very vivid. 'The lesson started with two separate groups of boys and girls (a very frequent occurrence), sitting rather at a distance from one another. When they were reading a short passage, and Richard was asked among others to read aloud, his answer was "Oh, not me again Miss." He read in a very bored and fed up way, conveying the feeling that he wasn't going to put too much of himself into it, and he made quite a number of mistakes. This is an important examination class, and I told him that he would find it quite difficult to get a pass if he didn't put a little more effort into this subject and that we should talk a little about his catching up. He answered in a sort of seductive and, I felt, rather offensive voice – "Yes Miss, your place or mine?" I was very taken aback and didn't say anything.

'Incidentally, Richard was sitting next to Michael, another fan of Genesis. They started talking with one another in a whisper, and I felt there was a very secretive quality in their behaviour. I found it very difficult not to ask *what* they were talking about. In fact, I did, and was told they were talking about Genesis.

'I was struggling with teaching the rest of the class the past tense of some French irregular verbs and attempted to involve Richard and Michael in the lesson by asking them some questions. Michael remained silent. Richard said that in order to learn French, one should not have to learn verbs in this boring way, that different and more interesting methods should be used. I said firmly, and perhaps a little angrily, that I had not asked him for advice about my teaching methods. Later in the lesson I asked Richard a very simple question. I was certain that he could answer it if he had paid the slightest attention. Richard could not be bothered or perhaps he really didn't know the reply to my question. He gave a half-hearted wrong answer. I lost my patience and said "Stop pretending you're stupid." Richard replied in a tone of offended innocence "Don't take it out on me, Miss." I felt very close to tears, rageful tears, because I realised that by losing my patience I had played into Richard's game and come down to the level he wanted to drag me. At the end of the lesson I said goodbye to everybody and left the class with considerable relief. Richard shouted after me in a way that reminded me of "your place or mine?" – "Don't you say goodbye to *me*, Miss?" I felt very irritated. Richard followed me into the corridor. He had a cassette in his hands and said: "Would you like to borrow this? We can make a bargain – I'll teach you to appreciate Genesis and, if you do, I will swallow your French verbs."

'I just said that I disliked bargains, but I felt taken completely off-guard and I was probably still feeling guilty because of my having previously lost my patience, so I accepted the cassette. As soon as I got home I knew I'd made a mistake. I felt so angry with myself (even more than angry with Richard) that I wasn't able to listen to all the tape (incidentally I *do* like some pop music, but not the Genesis pop group). I returned Richard's cassette in the following lesson. I didn't tell him whether I'd listened to it or not, but only that we had to find a way of working at his 'O' levels which wasn't based on any sort of bargain.'

This presentation confronted us with a very large spectrum of problems and I would like to refer to some of the points which emerged in this discussion.

Mrs T had obviously found herself in what I referred to as the 'wedge game' in the previous chapter. Mr S, the substitute teacher, had been perceived by the 15-year-olds in the class as an older adolescent. (Of course we know little about his actual behaviour. We cannot rely on Richard, nor on the well-intentioned informer, Nadia, to have given an objective report.) This was highlighted by the remark that Mrs T was a 'middle-aged bird' who would be past pop music. It is very reminiscent of the way adolescent groups (some of them on the threshold of a gang formation) talk about parental figures. Everybody over 25 may be defined as middle-aged and past it (the frequent adolescent conviction that they have cornered the market of sexuality at the expense of the previous generation). It was obviously hurtful for Mrs T to be at the receiving end of these attacks. Fortunately, she looked like anything but a 'middle-aged bird', yet she said that she had suddenly felt somewhat decrepit and that she thought she might have made a mistake by accepting the cassette driven by a need to demonstrate that she was *not* 'past it'.

Another painful experience had taken place when Richard and Michael were talking with one another in a secretive way. A feeling of being the excluded small child, burning to know the 'secrets' that adults in general (parents in particular) whisper to one another or keep behind a closed door at night, can be revived in any of us at any age. Mrs T's impulse to ask Richard and Michael what they were talking about could perhaps be understood in terms of the infantile feelings that were evoked in her in that situation. This experience was reinforced by her feeling attacked and de-skilled in her *adult* role as a teacher by Richard's calling her lessons boring. Mrs T told us that she could kick herself for her childish behaviour. I tried to stress the differentiation between the somewhat derogatory word 'childish' and the word 'child-like'. We can only prevent the child in us from making serious incursions into our adult life by acknowledging its existence (just as there is no life-tree without roots), by getting to know as much as we can about the way he or she feels and looking after this child so that it doesn't dominate our lives. This is certainly not achieved by ignoring it or denigrating it.

While Paul appeared to be a child trapped in self-idealisation, Richard's contemptuous attitude toward parental figures (for instance, teachers over 25) appears to be based on the *idealisation of a peer group*. We see him busy forming little 'anti-parent gangs' with Michael and with the substitute teacher. His attempt to treat Mrs T as a possible girlfriend ('your place or mine, Miss') and his invitation to agree on a bargain, runs along similar lines. He would even have been prepared to swallow French irregular verbs if this could be done on a peer basis of exchanging. In that case he would, in his mind, have been the richer and more generous partner, offering the delights of Genesis in return for boring French irregular verbs. Mrs T is invited to join the gang of the pop groups fans. (It would be easy to speculate on the attractiveness of the spectacular job description evoked by a word like Genesis.) Richard's bargain is spelled out in no uncertain terms; feelings of dependency are obliterated, so is the acknowledgement that Mrs T might have something to offer him which is more significant than notions about French grammar, i.e. not only her teaching expertise, but her concern for being instrumental to a learning process that goes well beyond French irregular verbs. Her attempts to engender any feelings of responsibility about the task in hand, not just the forthcoming exams, were doomed to fail while she was enmeshed, as she very clearly saw herself, in Richard's tactics. She said in the discussion that she had been caught off-guard by Richard's comment – 'Isn't the other chap here, Miss?' – she had really not expected such a reception. She could envisage only retrospectively, with the help of the group, that perhaps Richard might have been voicing on behalf of the class very mixed feelings evoked by her absence.

They had resented it no matter how 'smashing' (Richard's word) Mr S might have been. Somehow she had to be punished and indeed she was. One can detect considerable hostility also in the detailed report that the dutiful Nadia takes upon herself to convey to Mrs T all of Richard's derogatory remarks ('She's too old for pop music', 'a middle-aged bird'). These words were meant to hurt and indeed they did. Michael appears to be another willing member of the class/gang in joining Richard in belittling and denigrating Mrs T and making her feel at the lonely end of a triangle.

Very strong feelings were evoked in the group by Mrs T's presentation. Her courage in bringing us an instance where she 'had deeply disliked herself', enabled many other teachers to bring examples of similar occurrences. Many of them had been confronted at some time in their careers with a Richard-type of pupil. In the case presented by Mrs T, it appeared helpful to consider her absence from school at least as a contributory factor to the contemptuous behaviour with which she had been bombarded, but it was rightly pointed out by a member of the group that one could not extend this motivation to all circumstances where children behave in a contemptuous way. Some of them appear to be consistent and persistent in their denigratory attitude quite irrespective of holiday breaks or absences of a teacher.

A subject that came to the fore in connection with Mrs T's presentation and, in particular, in our discussion about the temptation to placate denigrating children and to bribe them, was the issue of the strong feelings evoked in the staff by children who do not seem to express contempt towards a particular teacher, but to extend it to the school as a whole by absenting themselves for long periods. Although the problems of truanting and school-phobic children may be very different, it became apparent in our discussion that many teachers felt tempted to bribe both truanters and school-phobic children into attending: 'To do a bargain with them' – to put it in Richard's terms. Mrs K told us, for instance, about Gillian, a 14-year-old absentee.

Gillian had been promised an Easter egg if she attended school for one consecutive week and she was granted all sorts of special concessions. For instance, she used at times to knock at the staff-room door during break saying that she was frightened of the other children. She was allowed in and, at times, she had coffee with the staff. I think this preferential treatment, far from diminishing her fear of her peers, might have increased it as it would inevitably evoke envy and hostility in the other children.

It appears that a very crucial adult task when faced with being devalued in one's role is to resist reacting to the painful feelings evoked by 'trying to devise the right commercial to sell a poor product'. First of all one might reflect on *one's own* assessment of the 'product' to be bought. Indeed criticism and even denigration can at times give us an opportunity to reflect on our work, to assess it or re-assess it and no doubt we may always find room for improvement. But the central issue is that one should not be concerned to improve the product merely in order to make it superficially attractive.

I wish to return to the parallel with the mother of a poor feeder. I think it is very relevant to be concerned about the acceptance of food (food for thought in this case) as necessary fuel for development rather than as a means of restoring one's self-confidence as a cook. Both Paul and Richard were in fact poor feeders and poor learners, and we have seen how, in both of them, an intolerance of dependence could be detected as well as a considerable amount of envy, a tremendous difficulty in accepting that someone might be richer and therefore capable of providing something enriching.

Envy as one of the driving forces in denigration

I would like to conclude with an example where a denigratory attack due to envy appears almost in 'pure culture'.

Before reporting Mrs N's notes verbatim, it should be noted that the lesson described took place towards the end of the school year. The children in Mrs N's class knew that she would be leaving the school in the summer to return to her home country.

'Gloria is a West Indian girl who was transferred from another form at the beginning of the year. I had taught her already in the previous year, and found her quite disruptive and difficult. She wouldn't sit down, would not try to work anything out for herself, and her favourite phrase was "I can't do it" or "I don't know". She needed a tremendous amount of attention, but wasn't really very rewarding in terms of making use of these attentions.

'Last Wednesday there were relatively few kids in class and the atmosphere was quiet and pleasant. We have been revising quite a lot of the year's work in preparation for a series of tests after Whitsun. Most of the kids were working by themselves and I was wandering around the class giving assistance here and there. Gloria was doing well and she several times asked for some help. Sitting behind her were two girls, Sandra and Lucy, who do extremely little work and whom I regard as my failures in an otherwise good and cohesive class. They were giggling and talking or just staring into space. I can't get them to either ask for help when they need it or even try the work. One of these girls, Sandra, had a lot of extra help last year and in fact showed a great deal of progress, but her willingness to work in my lessons has really disappeared. The other girl, Lucy, I find quite underhand and she prefers to withdraw completely and does virtually no work. Gloria was joining them in giggling and talking and they were generally hotting up the atmosphere, distracting Josephine who was sitting across the aisle and attempting to get on with her work.

'I went over to them and tried to encourage them to get some work done. I was leaning over a desk to speak to Lucy, and Gloria started running a comb through the ends of my hair which was hanging loose. I asked her to stop and said it hurt as it was tangled. Kids have often either commented on or touched my hair and I made nothing of it. Gloria kept on doing this until I was a bit annoyed and, after I had asked her for the third time to stop, she did so. Then she stood behind me and I could feel her lifting a strand of hair and saying: "Yes, it is very tangled, isn't it?" Then there was a peculiar silence and she sat down again. I turned and stood up and saw that Gloria had a sly smile on her face and that Josephine was also laughing; other girls were looking at me oddly too. I glanced at Gloria again and realised she didn't have the comb in her hand. As I ran my hands through my hair I found that she had taken a thick strand and wound it right round the comb. I said it was a horrible thing to do, but I wasn't yet too angry. I then tried to unwind the hair and realised that there wasn't any way I could do it and that I would have to cut the hair off. Gloria came up to me and said she could unwind it, she tried several times to take hold of the hair, all the while explaining she knew how to do it. I could feel the anger boiling up and I said that she had better go and sit down or I was going to get very cross. She did, looking a little alarmed, but also laughing and giggling about it. The others looked and felt a little embarrassed. I sat down and for a few minutes tried to untangle the hair, feeling extremely angry and hurt and trying to understand whether she had done it without realising that the hair would have to be cut. Finally I got a pair of scissors from my bag and cut off the hair, tossed the comb with the hair still around it at Gloria, and there was a little buzz of activity and comment as she took the strand of hair from the comb and raised it up almost like a trophy to show some other girls.'

As I have mentioned earlier on, the instance I quoted occurred very close to the end of the school year. Gloria had not been an easy pupil at the best of times, but her very contemptuous behaviour which was not in any way braced by the other girls in the class, her concrete attack on something beautiful (her teacher's hair), her success in making Mrs N feel 'tied up in knots and unable to think', as she told us, could partly be seen as an extreme example of the attempt to devalue and denigrate what is to be lost so as to avoid the painful feelings of missing it.

Undoubtedly this process of denigration is costly. While preserving the memory of someone valued could be enriching, but painful, denigration acts as an analgesic. The devalued teacher can be left behind in her tangle of feelings and hair (this was not fortunately what actually happened to Mrs N) and she could then be treated like Mary, the girl in Paul's drawing, i.e. she could be flushed away from everybody's mind. Indeed these processes are very depleting and might leave someone like Gloria feeling empty and hollow. T.S. Eliot beautifully describes the fringe benefits of the hollow state of mind in his poem 'The Hollow Men':

This is the way the world ends, this is the way the world ends,
this is the way the world ends, not with a bang but a whimper.

Chapter 7

Helpful relationships

In the previous chapters the risks of polarised relationships have been discussed. We have seen that a more helpful process can be initiated by a teacher when he or she stops colluding with being idealised or denigrated. This also often results in the teacher feeling more hopeful. As one teacher put it at a review meeting: 'I feel I have been given an "injection of hope" by this course.' The following examples may show how understanding helped to engender hope and modify for some of the teachers the perception of their job.

The hurtful child

Example (a): Mrs G presented a very vivid account of a 5½-year-old little girl, Vivian, who had recently joined her class, the second in the infants, having moved from a different school. She said that her first reaction to this child had been a very negative one and that she had questioned herself as to why she found it so difficult to like Vivian. She was struck by the child's ability to make other children feel inadequate and small. At times Vivian boasted about her talents and achievements (she happened to be the only child in the class working on a rather advanced reading book), and engendered in others a feeling of uncertainty about their abilities. Some perceived her presence as an impediment to learning; some worked less well than they had done the previous year before Vivian had joined the class.

On one occasion when Vivian had lost two of her crayons, she accused another child of having taken them and insisted on Mrs G punishing this child. This was one of the instances where the teacher had found it difficult to get close to the more likeable side of Vivian and experienced that this child was 'getting under her skin'. Mrs G also felt very uneasy when, at break-time, Vivian announced that she had brought sweets and then proceeded to select a few children she was going to give sweets to, excluding the ones who were particularly likely to be hurt – she appeared to have a sixth sense for perceiving this. All these aspects of Vivian's behaviour put across a clear picture of how she could deliberately set out to hurt others emotionally.

Mrs G also gave examples of Vivian's frequent physically violent behaviour. For instance, on one occasion, the teacher had to stop her beating one of the boys quite viciously. The boy in question was rather backward, cried easily and was very alarmed by Vivian's attack. Mrs G went on to give us examples of Vivian's boasting: for instance, she claimed her house was so large that everybody in the neighbourhood knew it and there was no need for it to have a number. The teacher added that she often felt Vivian couldn't stop herself and needed help in curbing her behaviour; she could sense that she was not by any means a happy child. For instance, on one occasion when Mrs G had pointed out that she frequently lost her belongings (the crayons had not been stolen, but lost), Vivian had burst into tears and seemed quite inconsolable. We discussed this outburst of tears at length. It seemed to be one of the very few examples of spontaneous behaviour that Mrs G could remember; on the whole, she had the feeling that it was very difficult for Vivian to let go, to smile or to laugh when she felt like it. Some people in the group were inclined to see Vivian's crying as a reaction to being reproached, as she seemed to need to keep up a perfect facade. Mrs G stressed that she had tried to get closer to this child and to talk with her in as gentle a tone as she possibly could. Wasn't there a possibility that Vivian felt understood when Mrs G, rather than seeing her as the perfect child on the advanced reading book, realised that she had difficulties in holding herself together and that her continuous losing of objects might be related to a feeling of precariousness? Mrs G was very much in agreement about the element of fragility in Vivian. She thought that this child felt that she was not likeable and yet could not stop herself behaving in a patronising and often hurtful way.

Vivian was discussed in our group on more than one occasion, and it was interesting to learn that, once Mrs G showed that she was more interested in her as a person, rather than simply in her as the clever child of the classroom, Vivian's achievements became less impressive. In fact, it looked for a while as if her reading ability had decreased. Mrs G told us that she had become very firm with Vivian, setting limits both to her emotionally and physically hurtful behaviour. She made it clear that she considered her no different from the others. She would, for instance, no longer be allowed to do something out of turn, like painting when the rest of the class were reading a book. She was expected to take part in everybody else's activities. Although, at first, Vivian seemed rather angry, Mrs G also perceived a feeling of relief in her, especially at being gradually able to drop the effort of 'having to be top all the time'. She noticed that Vivian was more capable of behaving spontaneously and, occasionally, when frustrated or upset, would cry. This contrasted with her previous skill in bringing tears to other children's eyes.

This example gave us an opportunity to discuss how often children who are unable to tolerate pain themselves, behave in an extremely painful way to others, peers and teachers alike, i.e. they put their own pain into others. The less a child is capable of bearing pain the more he tends to inflict (project) pain. Mrs G said that she had at first perceived Vivian as a very hurtful child and it was this which had got under her skin. The very significant help she gave this little girl consisted in her tolerating the painful feelings evoked by her behaviour and attempting to understand them rather than unthinkingly reacting to them. She said, for instance, that she had to make a considerable effort not to become punitive to Vivian, when she was being asked by her to crack the whip and punish the other child. She said that the instance of the crayons reminded her of the distress evoked in her when her 3-year-old daughter, Carol, had quite fiercely pinched her 6-month-old little brother. She said, 'All my mother-hen feelings came to the fore, maybe because I teach little ones.' Other members of the group involved in secondary or tertiary education, however, commented that equally strong feelings had been evoked in them by much older students who behaved in a manner similar to Vivian's.

The hurtful child is very likely to engender a need to protect the rest of the class and this can be achieved by firmness rather than punishment. The temptation to become punitive can be very strong and can only be counteracted by allowing space for thought rather than reacting impulsively. One can well imagine how unhelpful it would have been to Carol if her mother had pinched her in order to 'teach her a lesson', rather than attempting to understand her obvious jealousy in a more soothing way. It may be relevant to add that the temporary decrease of Vivian's reading ability was not perceived by Mrs G as her failure as a teacher. If the main motivation for being academically brilliant is the one of engendering envy in other children and making them feel inadequate, it not infrequently happens that, when this pattern is not colluded with, a student *temporarily* loses some of his drive for learning. Hopefully he might gradually be helped to find a healthier motivation; last but not least a pleasure in learning.

Just as Mrs L, in the chapter on idealised relationships, was delighted when Tina decided to drop one of the many subjects she had planned to take for her exams, Mrs G was not disheartened by the temporary decrease in Vivian's academic performance. Such an attitude implies an important shift in terms of a teacher's priorities. It means that the teacher doesn't feel that the only honest way of earning one's wages is by promoting academic standards, regardless of the emotional development of the student and the social relationships in the classroom. We saw, in fact, how Vivian's boasting about her talents engendered considerable feelings of inadequacy in other children and even interfered with their learning.

It is, of course, well beyond the task of the teacher to explore the motivation for learning in all instances, but where there is clear evidence for the need to attain special achievements the teacher may need to consider why the pupil is so driven by ambition. Here is another case which will illustrate the point.

Example (b): Mr R, an English teacher, told us about Steven, a very bright boy, interested and doing well in English Literature. Steven was also quite a talented actor and placed great hopes on being cast as Othello in a school performance; instead he was assigned a minor role in the play. Steven had a great need to be in the limelight and his rage and disappointment were immense. He thought that Mr R was involved in selecting the actors (in fact this was not so), and for a while he 'went on strike', not handing in his essay on Othello. Fortunately Mr R was able to help Steven overcome his disappointment and eventually adopt a more co-operative attitude. He said this took him about two months of very, very hard work. He was glad he had the opportunity for individual talks with Steven at the time, when his grievances were at their height. Steven claimed that the boy cast as Othello had only been chosen because he was 'a nigger'. Mr R had reacted very firmly to this comment, saying that those were words worthy of Iago. He felt that Steven had then come to his senses and hopefully would not voice such a hurtful comment in class. The group felt that there were great similarities between 5½-year-old Vivian and 18-year-old Steven in terms of their need to be painful and hurtful to *another* because of the deep intolerance of their *own* pain.

The tyrant or slave child

Here is another case where containment of aggressive and hurtful behaviour was also very important, though the context is a very different one: Darren is a 14-year-old immigrant boy who had been truanting a great deal in the previous year and is now in his third year in secondary school. He was often violent with other boys and did not seem to have a preference for younger, older or boys of his own age. His reading and writing left a great deal to be desired, and he was still attending a remedial teaching class for part of the time. The teacher who presented was his form master and he wanted to discuss how he might deal with Darren's violent behaviour. Mr S told us that at his school corporal punishment was still used. He himself was very much against caning and therefore in conflict with the rest of the school staff. Darren had apparently been beaten as a very small child and Mr S had heard him boast that his father had beaten him so hard on one occasion that the broomstick had broken on his back. Mr S gained the impression that Darren showed some pleasure in describing this event and that he might, to some extent, also enjoy being beaten at school. Mr S told us that he was very doubtful about the type of relationship that Darren had established with his remedial teacher. He had made some progress but he thought that this was partly due to the fact that the remedial teacher was a very 'austere' person. He had said on more than one occasion: 'Make sure that Darren gets caned.' Mr S felt this to be very detrimental for this boy and intuitively perceived something unhealthy in Darren's capacity to bring about situations where he was at the receiving end of corporal punishment. He found it impossible to establish a close contact with this boy – it was in fact extremely difficult for anybody to do so. He often came to school with a transistor radio in his pocket, plugs in his ears and would sometimes listen to the radio even during lessons. It was this type of provocative behaviour which led to his being caned. Mr S had often been goaded by Darren, but had tried to put across to the boy that he felt it would not do him much good if he adopted a punitive attitude. Yet he found the boy put up a considerable barrier if he tried to reach him in any other way.

We discussed Darren's behaviour and the effect it had on others: being elusive and slippery, absent and out of touch, were the kind of feelings that he himself might well have experienced having been left by his parents and only rejoining them in England three years later. He might not have found it easy to come to a strange country and settle again into a family from whom he had been separated for a long time. It was worth thinking about whether these facts played a part in his attraction for violence, both in terms of his being at the giving and at the receiving end of it. Mr S felt sure that at least Darren did not perceive him as someone who would use the cane on him, and that this could be the basis for the development of whatever relationship Darren might be capable. Our discussion focused on how gradual the development of a capacity for trust might be for this boy. There was something in Darren's pleasure in being caned that was somewhat reminiscent of Vivian's request for another child to be punished (although not corporally). This made us consider the unhealthy phantasies that can accompany enjoyment of punishment, whether one's own or someone else's, and how it is important to contain and think about this pattern rather than collude with it. Mr S's attitude, his attempts to understand Darren's attraction only for relationships where he was either beating or being beaten, could, given time, be experienced as an offer for holding the cruelty and containing it.

The crucial question was why Darren appeared to be asking for a strait-jacket rather than for a container. Why was he putting across such a feeling of hardness?

Hearing about his history, there was little doubt that he had been exposed to painful experiences in his childhood; perhaps he had been exposed to more pain than he could digest – it left such deep scars that they had to be covered up. It is not infrequent in such cases that one of the ways to deal with the undigestible pain is to turn it into excitement, a 'pain-is-beautiful' kind of attitude. In this type of child or adult, it matters little whether one is the slave or the tyrant. We can see how, in Darren's case, there is a continuous fluctuation between the two. He also came across as a boy who had transferred the experience of pain from the mental to the physical level. He appeared to have abdicated his capacity to think and reflect, using the transistor radio plugs in his ears to blot out thought. He probably could not risk getting in touch with his feelings and memories.

This mindless attitude is common amongst children who have suffered deprivation and is often associated with learning difficulties. If important figures have disappeared and then suddenly re-appeared in their lives, they switch off and let others experience *their* unreachability. Mr S told us that this discussion helped him to understand the nature of Darren's elusive and slippery behaviour. He could only stand by and make himself available should this hard-to-reach boy, at some point, put enough trust in him to shed some of his protective layers and take at least one plug out of his ear.

A very heated discussion took place in the group on the issue of caning, a practice likely to reinforce Darren's pattern of defences and defeat Mr S's attempts to reach him. While agreeing with the difficulty of the predicament, I found I had to make a considerable effort not to join the group in a crusade against corporal punishment. I felt that we were at risk of falling into the trap of perceiving ourselves on 'the side of the angels', forgetting that Darren's problems might have been reinforced, but certainly did not originate from the use of the cane. Our primary task was to help Mr S help Darren, and not to give fuel to his resentment towards his colleagues. We had a perfect example in the dynamics of the group, of how violence breeds violence as the discussion developed at one point into what could be expressed by a slogan such as 'Death to caners'. It was very helpful for us all to observe what was happening in the group, attempt to understand its meaning and struggle to contain the feelings evoked in all of us.

The empty child

Mrs L presented Julian, beginning with these words: 'He is a very silent child, he never moves. The observation I am bringing today could be that of any other day. He sits down and smiles when I talk to him in a way that reminds me of the smile of Leonardo's Mona Lisa.' It is a very enigmatic, distant smile, but there is also something very gentle about it. Mrs L had decided to focus on this child in particular, because he is the one who escapes notice as he does not make himself heard, and puts across a feeling of not wishing to be noticed. She wanted to try and think about him because she was concerned that he was so withdrawn.

Mrs L takes a class of 10-year-olds which has a high proportion of immigrant children in it. She said that many of the chidren give her a feeling of being very uncertain about their identity. She had been advised by a colleague to ask the children to describe themselves, making a kind of identity card for themselves. In answer to the question: How would you describe yourself?, Julian had written: 'My mother says that I am generous.' The teacher was struck by this very atypical answer, his sense of identity seeming to be carried by what his mother thought of him. Julian agreed to write another identity card and his words were: 'I am silent in class and also at home, I am very shy and nervous, maybe I am a little intelligent, I am not generous, not interesting, I am very tidy and have no courage.'

Mrs L reported that she felt guilty because she didn't give Julian enough attention. She would ask him a question and when he didn't answer at once and other children started talking, she turned to another child rather than waiting for an answer from Julian. Julian had often a vacant look in his eyes, giving the impression that he was 'empty inside'.

It was on this question of emptiness that our discussion centred. Was this really a child who had nothing inside, nothing to say for himself, and wanted to be left alone, pass unobserved; or was this behaviour a defence against being aware of himself, avoiding having a mind to think or to be in touch with his feelings? If so, was it right to try and force a child who so needed to protect himself to become more alive? One teacher commented that one shouldn't allow anyone alive to be so dead to the world. It seemed important not to use a forceful approach in depriving Julian of his defences; it might, however, be useful to make oneself available and open to any possibility of contact with him. Perhaps, rather than being empty, he may be wrapped in a sort of protective layer. We didn't know of course what scars might be under this protective layer. Mrs L remembered at this point, that, on one occasion, Julian had actually spoken of an incident at home; he had scalded himself and had shown the teacher a scar on his arm. The teacher had told him she knew how painful it was when one got burned, and showed him a scar on her hand which had also been caused by a burn. In the ensuing discussion teachers wondered whether it was right to say something so personal, but most thought that it was important for a child like Julian that Mrs L could say: I know how it feels. As the discussion progressed, it became apparent that in fact this child was not at all indifferent to her, but that she had often felt impelled to collude with his wish to be ignored.

We heard about Julian in subsequent presentations and Mrs L told us that it was very useful to ask him to help handing out things in class. He seemed to respond with great pleasure and to carry out his tasks in an efficient way. He was still slow in his work and the impression he gave was of someone 'under anaesthetic'. Mrs L said that, since our discussion about him, she had become much more receptive to any indication Julian gave of wishing to participate. On one occasion he had taken part in a discussion, but seemed unable to talk to the point – his remarks were somewhat off the track and rather conjectural. She had not interrupted him as she might have done in the past; she had let him speak because she knew that this was such a new experience for him that his first attempts were bound to be somewhat clumsy.

The patchwork child

The same teacher, on a different occasion, presented Joseph, a child who appeared to have some similarities to Julian. She said that she would find it helpful to compare these two children. Joseph was described as always arriving at his lessons with an enormous bag, but one couldn't figure out what was in it. He never brought his exercise books, he always used bits of paper which he subsequently lost. He never respected the spaces on the paper when he was writing and was extremely slow. Mrs L said that he was not quite 'together'. This was also true in terms of his clothes; he often wore short trousers (even in winter) and a very heavy anorak that he never took off. She said he looked like a 'patchwork child'. He used to write with a blunt pencil but didn't bother to sharpen it, thus making very heavy marks on the paper; on one occasion he said that he needed better paper because the sheet he was given was too thin and kept tearing. He appeared to be as fragile as the paper he complained about. For instance, on one occasion his pencil fell into a slit in his desk and he couldn't get hold of it and started crying. At the beginning of the year he had often been in tears. The group discussed whether it was a good sign that Joseph could cry in class or whether his crying less now was a sign of improvement. His teacher appeared to feel that he had gained more trust in his relationship with her, and although he seemed at times to be all over the place and in need of binding (very much like his pieces of paper), there were other moments when he had responded with incredulous gratitude when given individual attention.

On one occasion Joseph gave the teacher something of which he was very proud. He excelled at woodwork and this was linked to his father's profession of cabinet-maker. Joseph had brought Mrs L some spoons that he had carved and showed them to her with great pride. While the teacher was admiring them some of the children said in a very spiteful way that all Joseph could do was to work with his hands as he had nothing in his head, and they mocked him for being 'thick'. This is where a firm attitude was most helpful. The teacher protected Joseph by saying that she very much liked his work. She spoke about different types of wood and their merits in terms of carving. Joseph was most responsive to her interest in a subject where he had some talent and knowledge. On the basis of this he had been able to develop more in other areas of learning and participate more in class.

Although there are similarities between Julian and Joseph, one feels that while the former could only very gradually come out of his shell, Joseph was craving to find someone who would reach out to him. He was much less frightened of a relationship, perhaps because he had fewer scars than Julian.

We have seen how children could respond in varying degrees to being understood. Not all children, however, can accept containment, even when they are badly in need of it. A very striking remark of a nursery school teacher comes to mind. Speaking about a solitary and miserable little girl of 3 years, severely affected with eczema, she commented: 'Her skin is so cracked that although I often feel a strong impulse to pick her up and hold her on my lap, especially when we sit in a circle having milk, I feel inhibited – even holding her could be hurtful, her skin is too sore.' Such children may require specialist help – and even then the outcome is by no means certain.

Part IV

Work with families and professional colleagues

E. Osborne

Chapter 8

The teacher's relationship with the pupils' families

Most of the chapters of this book are concerned with understanding the relationship between teacher and student or pupil, with the factors which can facilitate or hinder learning within the environment of the school. The authors hope to increase the teachers' own understanding and ability to deal with the problems that arise and to encourage practices that seem most helpful.

There will, nevertheless, be times when the teacher will need to be in contact with other people who are concerned with their pupils. These may be professional colleagues from many different agencies and in the case of children at school it is most likely that this will include their parents. This part of the book is an attempt to deal with some of the issues that can arise.

The range of the problem

The need for good parent-teacher relationships is everywhere acknowledged and there have always been schools which were highly successful in this respect. The Plowden Report, published in 1967, was a milestone in junior school education, and it attached great importance to the way in which teachers related to parents. It described some of the best practices and attempted to codify these into a list of suggestions for all schools.

These included preparatory meetings before a child started at school, accessibility to class teachers as well as to head teachers, using open days not only to display the work of the school systematically, but to allow staff to make individual arrangements so that both parents might be encouraged to come; booklets about the school, including what work the parents might encourage the children to do at home; and reports which invited comment from the parents. The Plowden Report went on to say that efforts to contact parents who did not visit should be made, but the teachers should not become social workers. The report gave a full account of a successful project applying these principles.

I have had discussions with individual teachers over the years as an educational psychologist and with teacher groups, which have shown how these ideas are carried out in practice. I do know of school staffs who go much further in offering support to parents than anything described by the Plowden Report. For instance, the headmistress of an infant school to whom mothers turned for advice and help over many everyday problems of child development and management.

Some good practices, such as preparatory meetings for parents, are now common and others, e.g. reports which invite parental comment, are increasingly used. I have also heard of a number of interesting experiments, for example classes in new mathematics for parents, or mothers coming into school to help with reading groups.

My discussions with teachers have revealed considerable support for some of the Plowden proposals, but less for others. The reasons for this are therefore of some interest. It was often the case that individual teachers were not readily available to see parents making an unexpected visit, and the head teacher acted as a first contact. Instead of feeling resentful many teachers appreciated this protection and felt this left them free to get on with their primary task of teaching. There were also gains in having one person in the school with a detailed and ongoing knowledge of the family, the history of previous contacts and therefore more chance of dealing with requests, complaints or worries in an informed way.

Opinions on the value of home-visiting by teachers varied. In some cases it was clear that there were great advantages of informality, of greater awareness of the realities of a child's home background, and of meeting the family on its own ground. However, care was needed where child or parents, or both, felt the visit to be an intrusion into privacy.

Although open days often provide the main opportunity for parents to come to school, the teachers are aware of unsatisfactory aspects to these for those parents who need more time, or feel the situation is too public for a real discussion and therefore are disappointed. I recall an instance when a request was made at an open day for a child to be excused swimming, the parent explaining that the child was afraid. The teacher was aware that behind this request might be important implications, but there was no possibility to go on to explore these and the opportunity was lost. An alternative is to use the Open Day as an occasion when subsequent appointments can be made, and this has proved to be very productive.

Otherwise it is most likely that parents will be called in when there is a deteriorating situation. This is often the point at which the teachers attempt to initiate referral to a child guidance clinic or school psychologist. The following are two cases discussed with me where it had become clear that referral was not likely to receive co-operation from the parents but where interviews with the parents still gave the teacher concerned a basis for a new approach.

One teacher described to me a teenager causing concern through petty delinquency, whose parents had never previously visited the school. In response to an urgent request his father only arrived. In the ensuing discussion he described how the boy's mother was severely agoraphobic and could not move from the house. This longstanding problem and the resulting tensions at home made parental control difficult, and there had been no response to attempts to help the family. Although at the time the teacher felt helpless over any possibility of changing a situation quite removed from her own sphere of influence, she did find that she now had a greater understanding of the problems. This sympathy provided a basis for more certain control on her part, and this greater firmness was more helpful to the boy himself.

In another case a frail 10-year-old was doing especially badly in her reading. The parents and their daughter came together to see the head teacher and remedial teacher. In the course of the interview it was explained that mother had been very ill. Father said, 'We nearly lost Mummy.' Then, directing his remarks more specifically to his daughter said, 'Now you have got to learn to read to help Mummy.' This brief glimpse into the pressures at home gave the teacher an idea of the reasons behind the girl's resistance to reading, and subsequently into other aspects of her feeling about growing up and its consequent responsibilities, which modified the approach used by the teacher.

Two other examples from my work illustrate the usefulness of direct contact in preventing the playing off of home against school. In one case some parents complained angrily to their child's school over his bad reports. In discussion it emerged that the son told the parents that no homework was being set, although the parents themselves felt that this would be helpful to him. Concurrently the boy told his teacher that he had nowhere at home that he could do any homework, prompting the teacher into annoyance with the parents. There were major improvements when parents and teachers got together to agree on reasonable and consistent demands on the boy.

In the other case a girl drew her mother into collusion over her absences by getting her to write sickness notes. A series of meetings between the head teacher and the mother helped to strengthen the mother's resolve, and this led to improved attendance.

The parents' pleasure and gratitude in many of these cases, and their feelings that the teacher saw their child as valuable and important was often an unexpected bonus. Knowledge of a child's background could lead to more understanding, and this in turn meant that a teacher might make allowances, or act more decisively, co-operation could prevent 'playing off' and exploiting ignorances by a child, mutual misperceptions could be broken down.

In the area of classroom work teachers have described how explanations of likely achievement in the early stages of reading and number work can save much anxiety for parents, especially with a first child starting school. At the secondary level many examples have been given of parental misunderstanding of subject choices as well as ignorance of requirements for specific careers. Many of these problems could be clarified in a single session, but sometimes this was not sufficient for modifying deeper seated attitudes and teachers expressed disappointment that change was often so limited after what might have seemed a good discussion.

At times the nature of the rivalry between parents and teachers, arising from the desire of both to gain positive attitudes from the child, can be such that both sides avoid each other altogether. The parents unresolved feelings from their own schooldays, for instance feelings of fear or of rebelliousness which relate back to their childhood, may hold back or distort their contacts with the school staff. Parents may also be anxious about being criticised for shortcomings in the upbringing of their child on the one hand, whilst on the other hand teachers may anticipate being blamed for learning and discipline failures, which may either lead to angry exchanges or inhibit communication altogether. In such circumstances of mistrust the teacher may unwittingly enter into an alliance with the child's wish to demonstrate superior knowledge and skills in contrast to what are seen as the parent's old fashioned ideas.

Counselling an individual child requires particular tact and skill to maintain the child's trust in the teacher/counsellor at the same time as remaining acceptable to the parents also.

The following are rather more detailed cases from teachers discussion groups, and illustrate some of the difficulties that can arise.

The pursuit of facts

There are times when the desire to know and understand a home background can lead to a piling up of unusable facts about the family history or situation.

Tom was a 14-year-old truant. Wanting to understand him better his teacher made contact with mother and between them they discovered that he had lied convincingly at home about his activities at school, when he was not in fact there. Clearly, he had also lied at school about the reasons for his absences. The knowledge of the lies made the teacher feel he had no objective facts he could rely on, nor any true basis on which to build a counselling type of relationship. One of the facts uncovered early on was that the parents of this only son belonged to a particularly severe religious sect and the teacher's anger towards the boy's lies was somewhat modified by awareness of the strict atmosphere at home. Nevertheless, the teacher felt he had been subtly manouevred by the lies into an over sympathetic stance and was determined to 'get to the real truth'.

Within the discussion group, we also became dominated by the need to know facts, questions flowed fast and furious about the exact nature of the family, their religious beliefs, the sort of contacts they made, and how Tom would have been brought up and so on. The solutions proffered for the current situation also tended to emphasise the need for the truth, that home and school should be in touch over any absence, so that Tom could not 'get away with it'. The teacher should let Tom know that he was aware of the lies and should insist on having the truth. It was suggested that the leader of the church should be drawn in to help, although in fact nothing was known about him, nor how suitable this request would be.

Now of course all of this might have been potentially useful, but the punitive flavour suggested the possible beginnings of a witch hunt. Anyway by the end we were apparently no nearer to understanding the truancy from Tom's point of view than we were before and, therefore, we were in no position to speculate as to how he might respond to the actions suggested. At this point, feeling that sympathy was being lost and that we were perhaps running away like the truant from insoluble difficulties, I suggested that we might consider in detail the discussion the teacher had had with Tom, including the nature of the lies he had told. What emerged was a picture of a boy of moderate ability with ambitions for a professional career which were unlikely to be realised. Absences appeared to provide an excuse for failure and Tom thereby avoided the need to acknowledge his limitations and to embark on the painful search for alternative careers. The importance of his self-esteem and the attempt to establish his own identity could be related, in this context, to the difficulties for this adolescent in a restrictive, rigid home which allowed little in the way of exploration or experiment. One or two of the teachers were then reminded of their own preoccupations in adolescence and a new attitude emerged towards Tom, which was once more sympathetic yet realistic, and a plan could be made to give vocational guidance. The truancy remained an important factor against the background of a home unlikely to be much modified. Discussions on Tom's picture of himself became more important than insistence on the truth, and subsequently the teacher attempted to improve, just a little, the relationships at home rather than straight policing of Tom's absences. The desperation behind Tom's lies pointed to the importance of some individual counselling. Useful though background information about the home can be, we are liable at times to get carried away by the piling up of facts, which in the end can obscure from us the understanding which we were originally striving for.

Co-operation or collusion?

The second case is an example of another truant, this time a girl of 15, where co-operation with the home came close to collusion against the girl. Sharon had a longstanding pattern of occasional absences but otherwise had not especially attracted attention. Following a minor accident her house tutor (who had a counselling and teaching relationship with the girls in her house) took her to the hospital. During this time Sharon spoke of her home, presenting an unhappy story of divorced parents, and how her mother, having remarried, planned to divorce again. Sharon was upset about this and was having rows with her mother. The teacher, with justification, felt the home background was providing problems which needed investigation and arranged a meeting with Sharon's mother. From her she learnt that Sharon had fairly recently run away, stayed overnight at her boyfriend's flat, saying later that she had stayed with a girlfriend. Since then she had continued to spend evenings with him, making very little effort to conceal this.

Having shared their concern the two adults then planned to refer Sharon to the psychological services. In fact, perhaps not too surprisingly, Sharon did not keep her appointment, instead the mother became more and more dependent on the teacher, ringing her quite often about her problems. The teacher was increasingly uneasy about this, feeling not only that she was being drawn into too great an involvement with the mother, but that she was unable to make contact with Sharon, who now felt the teacher was on her mother's side. The teacher changed her tactics and now tried to influence Sharon to re-establish a 'good relationship' with her mother. One of her mother's complaints had been deep regret at the loss of what had previously been a close, intimate relationship with Sharon. The teacher hoped by this change in approach to get back herself to a more direct contact with Sharon, and to disentangle herself from Sharon's mother without upsetting her.

With hindsight it is easier to see how important it was for a mother with two unhappy marriages to cling to her daughter, but looking at it through the mother's eyes at that time the teacher was most concerned with Sharon's safety and the need to protect her. Of course the pressure to get away from home was recognised, but seen primarily in terms of running away from the tensions and rows to the glamour of a boyfriend's flat. A solution seriously considered was to invite Sharon to stay at the teacher's home, where she could be safe and helped to return home eventually. Even though this idea was abandoned fairly soon as being likely to appear to the mother to be rivalry by the teacher to be a better mother than she was, the feeling remained that what Sharon needed most of all was some perfect mothering and that only this could save her.

When the discussion group looked at the issues they had to make considerable effort to see them from Sharon's point of view. The response to a request in the group for a physical description of Sharon was a reminder to us of her adolescence, and as Sharon's attempt to break away from her mother's possessiveness became clearer, the teacher recalled how much more important the flat and the housekeeping role within it were to Sharon than was the boyfriend himself.

It was a slow job for the teacher who now set about re-establishing her contact with Sharon. It was also difficult for her not to feel frustrated and impatient with Sharon's unresponsiveness. During one of our discussions the teacher, with greater sensitivity, looked at their relationship as she felt Sharon might see it. Following this there was marked improvement in the situation at school. Sharon continued to spend time away from home but there was still contact between her mother and herself. The initial loss of trust in the teacher, when she was seen as siding with mother, the teacher's unrealistic aim, to intensify the relationship between Sharon and her mother, which was in opposition to Sharon's need to create some distance from her mother, even though this aim was based on genuine concern for Sharon, were factors it was not easy to see at the time but which are felt to have stood in the way of eventually getting a useful counselling relationship established.

Joining forces against a parent

Jane was an upper sixth former in a school with a high academic level. After considerable 'O' level success her work for 'A' levels was suffering through bad feeling at home between Jane and her mother. Almost a year earlier Jane's rather elderly father had died. Although quite a lot older than his wife, the actual death was a sudden and unexpected heart attack. It happened at a weekend when Jane was away, staying with friends. The bereaved family were left in considerable financial difficulties and had to live in very poor accommodation for some time, longing for the new flat which they had been promised, talking of little else. The teacher who told us about Jane had quite good previous contact with the home and knew that the father had been a foreigner, that mother's family had virtually ostracised her following her marriage, and the parents had therefore been rather isolated, dependent very much on each other and on their own children.

Towards the school staff the mother maintained a reasonable attitude and, indeed, was very grateful for assistance offered over the move to the new flat. According to Jane, during the rows with her mother she had been rebuked for her absence when her father died. Her mother felt that she did not care, that when she stayed late to do her studying at school, by special arrangement with her teacher, she was in fact enjoying herself in the disco or hanging about the streets. These were Jane's own reports, but there was no reasonable doubt that she had become the target of her mother's angry feelings. At the time of her practise A levels she had stayed for a few weeks at a teacher's home and this had increased the subsequent rows. Now the suggestion at school was that she should again move out of her home for the period of her A levels, but her mother was threatening that if she did she would not have her home again.

The school staff felt that they were rightly giving their first priority to safeguarding Jane's academic success and subsequent move to university, and were indignant that this priority was not shared by her mother. There was some wish to confront the mother with the harm she was doing to tell her that she would be to blame if Jane failed. On a visit to the home the mother apparently covered up the extent of the antagonism between herself and her daughter and expressed her opposition more mildly as reluctance to take up the offer for Jane to stay with the teacher whilst taking her exams.

At last the family moved to their new flat and there was a big anti-climax. Not only was it impossible for it to live up to all their dreams, but they now had no hopeful topic of conversation, nothing substantial to look forward to. This made the tension even worse and increased the feeling that Jane must be rescued from this situation.

The anger of the teachers, and indeed of the discussion group, towards the mother totally swamped the sympathy for the mother's loss of her husband, the anniversary of which was very near, to be followed perhaps by the loss of her daughter too. In this atmosphere suggestions that the mother might also have needs led to rather harsh suggestions, that she should get a job, be encouraged to take up handicrafts, urged to get out of the house more and generally pull herself together. The facts suggested that, above all, this was a mother who wished to keep her problems, and her grief, private and contained. She never attempted, for example, to check with the school on the truth of Jane's statements. She may well have felt the offer to Jane (to stay at someone's home) was not only making her troubles public, but showing her own provision for Jane to be inadequate. Moreover her desperate need to keep the goodwill of others and her vulnerability must have made the prospects of any confrontation too frightening for her to express her opposition more assertively to the school. The staff indeed were embarrassed by the fact that she brought them a present to thank them for their help over the house moving.

This story particularly illustrates the difficulties in facing grief and mourning which are so frequently met in the wider society. Angry feelings are a common component of grief, in this case the only safe target for her mother's angry feelings appeared to be Jane, and vice versa. In separating Jane and her mother the school could appear to be encouraging Jane to ignore, even deny, any sense of loss at her father's death, and to blame her mother for the subsequent upset. Not only was there a danger that on top of the mother's grief would be added guilty feelings at having driven her daughter away, but also that Jane herself might later feel very badly at leaving her mother alone and pursuing her own interests; one subsequent possibility could be eventual anger with the school.

The school asserted its own priority, its high valuation of academic success, but in this case overlooked the importance for Jane's future development of coping satisfactorily with the consequences of her father's death and establishing a new relationship with her mother. The opportunities for taking her A levels would not be lost forever; the opportunity for Jane to establish her independence gradually and without long-standing bitterness might be spoiled indefinitely. It is certainly more difficult for a single child with one parent to achieve this. The possibilities of extreme solutions, i.e. on the one hand feeling so responsible for the parent as to be unable to move away at all, or on the other hand having to make a complete rejecting break, are already greater than in a two parent family. Jane's mother was being pushed into expressing her need to have Jane at home in a negative, threatening way, exacerbated by seeing her as the one who had been, and was still being, protected from the feelings of grief, with whom she could not share her sadness.

The teachers at school had explained the situation as one in which the mother was envious of Jane's youth, of her growing sexuality and new chance in life and therefore determined to deny her her freedom. It does seem very likely that these aspects were indeed present, but the action which was contemplated was, in a way, a confirmation that Jane did not have to live with the unpleasant feelings, should be protected from them at all costs, free to live and achieve the success predicted for her.

In the discussion group too, it was easier to share these feelings of faith and hope in life rather than to be caught up in thinking about death. Teachers especially devote their working lives to the young and their hopes for their future. In Jane's case this seemed to be taken to unhelpful extremes.

Two sides of the picture

Having dwelt at some length on Tom, Sharon and Jane, and the difficulties which arose, it may now seem as though the good intentions which lie behind attempts to know the home background of pupils has been undermined. Yet, of course, even a single visit from a parent can put right a whole set of distortions.

This is not to say that sometimes the child does not truly represent his background or, on the other hand, he may try to preserve a picture of an ideal home and keep discords and deprivations to himself. In Tom's case there is no doubt that it was useful to understand the limitations placed upon him by a materially well-providing but over-restricting home life. The most relevant question is not whether one is drawn into being too sympathetic or unsympathetic but how to deal with the feelings aroused in a way that will help the youngster to cope constructively with the good and bad aspects of his own life, which may include trying to change some of them, but to accept that, nevertheless, life is seldom exclusively black and white. Without this the aims set may be unrealistic e.g. to recreate the 'perfect' relationship between Sharon and her mother, or to rescue Jane and create an environment for her of complete peace, with all worries set aside.

In identifying or sympathising totally with the young person the teacher/counsellor may be drawn into a collusion against the parent, but it can sometimes happen the other way round, that together parent and teacher can, in the name of co-operation, act together against the child, or at least in such a way that the child's trust and confidence is lost. Both of these situations have been described. In Tom's case the teacher's attitude was dominated by the discovery that he was a plausible liar. Feeling betrayed by Tom he then saw the lies not as a symptom but as a disease in themselves. This created the rather persecuting attitude which hindered the use of the potentially helpful and informative contact with home.

In Sharon's case the teacher was drawn by the mother into denying Sharon's adolescence, although the shared concern for her well-being was quite genuine. Sharon's response to her mother had been to exaggerate her grown up independence by setting up home for herself, and the teacher was left helpless to intervene.

The primary concern with examination success of an academically high flying school does not often lead to such extreme action as in Jane's case. There is, however, a not uncommon attitude which demands that the students be protected and cocooned away from life's stresses (because of the need to devote all their resources to study), rather than learning with affectionate support to manage them.

My aim has been to explore some of the complexities which lie behind contact with parents and make success more than a matter of good intention. Yet it is also likely that an ongoing exchange within a tradition of shared concern, and mutual respect, because efforts had been consistently made by a school to involve their pupil's parents, would have eased the task of the individual teacher/counsellors in the cases described.

Influence of home versus school

There has been a great deal of debate, and some research, in recent years following a collapse in the belief that education could compensate for the shortcomings of a deprived home or a poor environment. This was especially marked in the USA following the bitter disappointment over the famous Headstart programme, but various reports in Britain during the decade from 1965 suggested that the possibility of reversing the influence of discouraging parental attitudes was minimal.

Later studies have done a great deal to modify this pessimistic view, with the discovery that schools with the same kind of catchment area could have very different records of success in their children's achievements and behaviour. The active involvement of the school staff in the community and in establishing contact with parents, so that teachers could be aware of the attitudes and problems at home, have been found to be important features of the schools which were successful, even though they were in a poor area, with high rates of delinquency and social problems.

Many teachers, however, are still suffering from the earlier loss of confidence in the effectiveness of education. For some, especially in the secondary schools, feelings of helplessness and discouragement have not yet been anything like sufficiently assuaged by these later, more optimistic findings. In such a situation a confident approach to parents is unlikely.

The reverse picture, when parents feel that everything can be left to the school, which is also quite common, is no more helpful. The best practices suggest that the good school recognises the importance of the home, does not expect to take the place of the parents, and accepts that its own role is different but also important. In encouraging more contact between the two I do not suppose that they must share everything. The children themselves can benefit from recognising that difference, perhaps finding relief in the less intense emotional atmosphere of school, or discovering a new kind of relationship with adults who are not primarily substitute parents and with a group of peers who are not siblings.

The security that a child obtains from knowing that his teachers and his parents value each other provides a firm base from which to explore, experiment and learn. Therefore I have been concerned as an educational psychologist to encourage such mutual respect between parents and teachers, and will illustrate this in the chapter on the school's relationships with child guidance teams.

Chapter 9

The teacher's relationship with other professional workers

This is the second of the two chapters in which the focus shifts from the teacher's relationship with an individual pupil to that which a school staff has with others who have a professional responsibility for a young person's welfare. Generally schools are the first line of help for a child outside of their family.

There will, nevertheless, be occasions when referral to an outside agency will be considered by a school staff. This may be in the expectation of additional or specialist facilities not ordinarily available in the school, or it may be made as part of a search for alternative placement, in a special school or other unit.

Special education

Although there is a move towards integration of handicapped children in ordinary schools, there will almost certainly remain a small proportion (the official estimate is about 2 per cent) who will need provision in special schools. Many such children will have severe physical handicaps which will already have been discovered. It is most likely that teachers will be concerned with borderline cases of physical handicap, where it has been agreed that child and school should try to adjust to each other. This border may be pushed back as new ways are found to help such children work in an ordinary classroom. In any case it is likely to include some children with invisible handicaps, e.g. hearing loss or diabetes where expert help will enable the teacher to know what allowances to make and what demands are reasonable.

A more sizeable problem for the teachers is likely to lie around those who fail to learn and those who are emotionally disturbing to themselves and others. The question of whether or not to seek for a place in a special school is likely to be addressed to the School Psychological Service. The

124

teachers may be asking for a clear-cut decision as to whether or not a child is educationally subnormal or maladjusted, and therefore beyond their scope as teachers of 'normal' children. Certainly the psychologist or the Child Guidance Clinic can help towards an answer, and their statement about the child will be crucial in obtaining a placement. Schools vary in their capacity to manage exceptional children and there are few general-isations that can safely be made. One that I would make from my experience is that primary schools sometimes refer children with special difficulties whom they are managing quite well, but where the referral is in anticipation of the transfer to secondary school. This is on the basis that a special school is more likely to reproduce the relatively protected atmosphere of the primary school than a large and confusing comprehen-sive could possibly offer. The 1981 Education Act attempts to do away with categories of handicap and to concentrate instead on the actual needs of any particular child. These will have to be matched against what is available, of course. The assessment of these needs by the relevant professionals will certainly require co-operation and careful observation by the school staff. In spite of regular review, transfer to a special school is very likely to be for the rest of a child's school life, and is, therefore, a very serious decision to take. It is only to be made when it is quite clear that ordinary schooling is no longer possible.

Medical and social services

Issues about where to refer are especially likely to arise when there is no clear focus for a child's problems, in their medical or psychological condition, in their family circumstances or their environment. Where there is any question of a medical problem then first recourse will almost certainly be to family or school doctor. It may be, however, that some medical conditions are not so easily recognised. As a psychologist it is necessary to be alert to the child with learning difficulties who has partial hearing loss for example. It is also very important for teachers to know what the effects of medical treatment, especially drugs, might be on a child's performance at school. On the other hand the results of neglect may be a matter of equal concern to the Social Services as to a medical clinic. This would apply to more violent cases of child abuse also, of course, but there is no doubt that many such children are picked up in hospital accident centres.

This brings me to one of the most crucial factors in making a decision to refer a child; that of parental co-operation. Where parental anxiety about referral to psychological services is very high it might help if the parents could meet first with the psychologist at school, with the referring teacher present. This would provide an occasion for the parents to ask questions about the referral and for the psychologist to get sanction from both school and parents to continue. Sometimes it may be necessary to raise parental anxiety where a child's difficulties are dismissed by a parent as unimportant, although, of course, this too may be an indication of considerable underlying anxiety. It may be that the decision to seek referral will, in itself, come as a shock to the parents, and they will need to be given some time to come to terms with it. If, in spite of careful discussion and preparation, a parent still refuses co-operation, then only in the most serious cases can referral be pursued, with the aim of seeking placement by statutory means for instance. Such decisions are especially difficult to make where behaviour problems are the main area of concern, and these are where a child guidance team are likely to be called upon.

The child guidance team

Although most areas did not have Child Guidance Clinics until the 1950s and 60s, it is possible to speak of a firm tradition, including a traditional child guidance team. This has consisted of a child psychiatrist, an educational psychologist and a social worker – many of whom still prefer the specialised title of psychiatric social worker. Often it also includes a child psychotherapist, and perhaps a remedial teacher or a speech therapist.

Each of these professions has also traditionally had its own circumscribed areas of concern. In recent years these have become more blurred, the focus on the individual child still valued but less routine, and the main responsibility for making decisions more likely to vary from one member of the team to another, according to the nature of the case. The educational psychologist has retained the major role as liaison to schools and in psychological testing, and is therefore the school's most likely contact with the team. The strength and special nature of this EP/school link has led generally to the separate establishment of a School Psychological Service, although the educational psychologists involved will still usually have access, maybe through a shared appointment, with a local Child Guidance Clinic.

Other members of the team may also have contacts elsewhere; for example the psychiatrist may relate to a hospital unit, the social worker to colleagues in the Social Services Department and so on. Much of what follows, however, is written from the particular point of view of an educational psychologist, but first I should mention some of the other services available.

When to refer for specialist psychological help

One of the advantages of not seeing clinics only as a final resort when all else has failed is that discussion around the issue of referral may be held in an atmosphere where the family may still feel it has some choice. If agreement is then reached the family will be far more likely to attend a clinic and to do so with a higher degree of motivation. I have known many head teachers successfully encourage a family to make its own referral at this point. Even if this does not happen, a rejection of the proposed referral may increase a family's determination to mobilise its own resources and to manage better for itself. Improvement may well follow.

One question to be asked is whether there is any desire for change in the child or family which can be built upon. If not, it may be necessary to wait for a moment of crisis, a moment when change of some sort may be, in any case, imposed. At such times a new pattern may be possible, if intervention can be swift and positive. This is especially true for adolescents, when the pace of development is rapid and the adolescent impatient.

Another useful question to ask before referring a child is whether there is an area of mismatch that could profitably be explored. An educational psychologist's tests may be one way of looking at the match between intelligence and attainments. A family interview may be concerned with the difference between school performance and parental expectations, or the match between the school's and the parents' standards. Looking at a problem this way may help the school staff responsible to decide what the focus for referral should be, including the question of whether the whole family should be encouraged to be involved.

Assessment at school

It is increasingly the case that assessment of a child's problems is made by co-operation between the teacher and the psychologist. Either of them might carry out brief but sustained and detailed sessions of observation; even ten minutes may be very instructive. Giving some thought in advance as to which interactions might be most relevant could lead to a choice of whether to include the playground, lunch time, different classes or different times of day. Comparisons may be most helpful and such an approach may be especially useful where there are conflicting views of a child.

In some cases a teacher may revise a view of a child when asked to make such close observation, with some specific questions in mind. For example a girl of 8 was reported as failing to make real progress in her work in spite of the fact that she seemed a cheerful, outgoing girl, bright and very friendly towards the teacher, who was puzzled and somewhat defeated by her. Following some close observation, the teacher then noted that the girl was also impatient and hasty, that her contacts with other children were bossy and self-willed. Rather than a self-confidence which could assist her work, she appeared to have an omnipotent belief in herself which actually got in the way of her accepting that she really needed to learn anything.

In making an assessment a teacher may make use of some more formal guides, attainment tests, checklists or classroom profiles. These are especially likely to be used for screening and therefore may select out children likely to develop problems, not yet evident.

Another way in which the psychologist may work with a school is by an arrangement to meet regularly with the staff. One possible task for such a group would be prior discussion of possible referrals. This is not without problems, as was shown when a clinic's offer was made for such a group to a school which was sending ill-defined referrals somewhat indiscriminately. Regular monthly meetings were agreed and this had an immediate effect in improving the amount of relevant information about the children concerned and of ensuring that differing views could be heard. It was also possible to advise on how parents should be consulted. However, the two clinic staff concerned had a hard time, especially in the first months, as the school staff discovered that not all the cases they brought could usefully be sent to the clinic, and became angry and frustrated about this. Subsequently some of the underlying difficulties within the school were revealed. The school had been through a major period of transition, with much disturbance, including staff changes, and the importance of this in the sudden spate of referrals became apparent. Apart from a drop in referrals, the school took back many of its problems and the staff used the discussion group to look at more general concerns, for instance truancy or the integration of a handicapped child.

Making contact with a school

Even as a professional worker, entering a school for the first time can be slightly unnerving. As a newly qualified educational psychologist it was a special pleasure when I was clearly expected, greeted by name and shown to the head teacher's room. Many other times I arrived, with no directions to the head teacher's room, nobody available to refer to, and would be left with the feeling that I was an intruder, or at best that the welcome given to visitors was a very grudging one.

When I got to know the schools better it was sometimes possible to uncover some of the feelings behind this cool greeting, the need to put a defensive screen between the school and the world outside. On the other hand school staff have often complained that they do not get sufficient information back from clinics or social workers.

If both sides want communication, what is the nature of the barriers which seem to make it so difficult so often? In particular, what are the emotional factors involved? It is true that timetables for all the relevant workers are overcrowded, that it is difficult to arrange to release teachers from immediate teaching responsibilities to join a discussion, and that many head teachers' policy of availability means constant interruptions. However, where there is conviction that the meeting is important, time can be found, the head teacher's door can be shut and the telephone turned off or intercepted.

The following cases attempt to illustrate some of the emotional issues which have seemed to be important, the rivalry, the fears of unreasonable demands or of blaming, anxieties about sharing confidential material about families. There may be misunderstandings about the nature of therapy, the meaning of the test results and feared disagreements about the importance of each other's role with regard to the child and the family.

Rivalry

This may be expressed in terms of competition for the child's attendance. If long-term therapeutic sessions are suggested then the loss of lesson time will be of great concern, since much treatment is bound to be offered during the school day. Child and parents may get drawn into a dispute and feel under pressure from both sides. It will also be open to the family to exploit such a situation to express their own ambivalent feelings about the need for therapy or the inadequacy of school.

In the following case this became a very important factor in the breakdown of therapy. Mrs Y was a widowed mother, with a busy, professional job, and a 9-year-old son, Michael, an only child. Mrs Y had been very much opposed to any contact with the school, although she had agreed quite readily to psychotherapy for her son. Mrs Y was a sophisticated woman, who had been able to acknowledge that her husband's death some years previously had been very traumatic for Michael and was largely responsible for subsequent problems. During Michael's therapy Mrs Y was seen only very occasionally, and she undertook to keep the school informed about Michael's absence from school for his sessions. For a time this seemed to work quite well, until Mrs Y began to press more and more for Michael to change the time of his appointments to after school hours, reporting pressure from the school as her main reason. Eventually she agreed that the psychologist might visit to explore the school's request, and the teacher confirmed how worried she was about Michael's progress. Although he was a bright boy she described him as one of the worst readers in the class. She then expressed quite a lot of anger about the clinic's lack of co-operation and it became apparent that Mrs Y had been sharing with her a great many doubts about the usefulness of therapy, her concern that Michael was missing some schooling, and the great importance she attached to academic studies.

It also became clear that Mrs Y had succeeded in promoting a considerable sense of rivalry between school and clinic as the psychologist found herself hotly defending the value of paying attention to Michael's psychological needs, whilst the teacher had taken over the task of pressing for a change of time.

From the therapist's point of view Michael had a special need for certainty, consistency, reliability, continuity and firmness, and she was reluctant to make changes, apart from the difficulties this would make in her own timetable. Michael himself was caught up in the conflicting loyalties and was not able to make a full commitment to therapy nor work for his teacher at school.

The teacher and psychologist had not met before and it took some time to unravel what had happened, to acknowledge the genuine quality of each other's concern and to think about the impact on Michael. In this the goodwill of the headmistress played an extremely important part. The pressures on Michael were eased and this allowed Mrs Y's underlying ambivalence about her son's need for therapy to emerge. Her feelings of failure in having an emotionally disturbed child, her inability to solve his problems by herself when she had previously attached so much importance to managing after her husband's death, and to keeping her own career going. The competition between school and clinic was used to mirror her own mixed feelings about this, alongside her ambitions for her son to be successful.

In contrast, where the contact between school and psychologist was well established on a basis of mutual respect a similar problem was very quickly resolved. In this case a very conscientious mother also felt badly about accepting her little girl's need for clinic help, but had been meeting another clinic worker regularly, together with her husband, and had been able to explore these feelings. Problems arose when the parents' worker left and there was a gap before they could pick things up with someone else. Again strong requests came to change times, so as not to interefere with school work, the parents reporting that this was at the insistence of the teacher. In this case a brief visit by the psychologist was enough to discover that the teacher had indeed said that she would, of course, prefer the child to miss as little school as possible, but this had been when prompted by the mother, and in fact the school remained very positive towards clinic help. The backing of the teachers subsequently in discussing the problems for the parents in making the choice between school and clinic time was invaluable.

It does sometimes puzzle teachers when the person who turns up at the school is not the therapist. It has been part of the traditional role of the psychologist to act as a link for the Child Guidance Clinic with schools, and within the clinic to remind the team of a school's point of view. The teaching background of most educational psychologists gives them some understanding of the teacher's position and priorities. Moreover they share a common interest in cognitive ability and achievement, in the use of tasks, which may often be an indirect way of dealing with anxieties, and an understanding of the school as providing a stable feature in children's lives, sometimes the most reliable one.

There is also an advantage in having one person from the clinic to provide continuity in contact. Finally, the therapist may prefer not to visit a school because of the difficulty this might make for the child in keeping these two experiences distinct, and in maintaining confidence in the therapist's discretion about confidential material.

Anxieties about confidentiality

In cases like the first one described, where referral was not made by the school and contact over the child is refused, the teachers are placed in a very difficult situation, whether the child concerned is presenting problems in school or not. Clinic staff will usually try to persuade the parents that contact is necessary and try to understand what the reservations are about. Quite often this will turn out to be anxieties about family background information which they do not want revealed anywhere else, and reassurances about this are necessary. Sometimes, when it is eventually shared, it is only to discover that much of it was known, or half known anyway, all along. The suspicion that information is being withheld may, therefore, sometimes be true, and will almost certainly be resented.

One way of allaying parental anxieties may be to discuss very fully with them what is going to be reported at school, or even perhaps to invite them to a shared interview. This may include the child in some circumstances, but generally children prefer not to be brought in to an interview at school between psychologist and teacher. On the whole, as commented before, children do want to keep clinic sessions private and separate, to the extent that we suggest teachers do not request information from them about their visits. Even quite mild questions, such as 'did you have a nice time?' may be experienced as embarrassing.

Some teachers do feel shut out by this rejection and, of course, many have a natural curiosity about what is happening. They all, legitimately, need to know whether progress is being made. It is not easy for the psychologist to convey all aspects of therapy; how what may seem like play may often involve very painful feelings, and be rightfully described as hard work. Sometimes the symbolism of the play has, however, illuminated a child's behaviour at school, as when a boy of 6 was spending much of his time clambering in and out of boxes, which could be related to his anxieties about being contained and held sufficiently.

131

Teachers vary in their understanding of how expression work can help to release and, at the same time, contain all sorts of feelings. Such help may come from the more academic syllabus too; literature and history would provide the clearest examples. As adults we may use the theatre in a similar way. The concepts of unconscious phantasy, transference and interpretation are more difficult to convey and examples out of context may seem strange and incomprehensible.

An occasional teacher will sometimes try to pick up and adopt what they feel is a comparable therapeutic approach for a child in treatment. At its extreme this can result in considerable confusion. At the request of a therapist I visited a school at a time when she was finding it very difficult to maintain the sessions. A warm, interested, infant school teacher showed me, with some amusement, the paintings of a child in therapy. They showed a witch-like woman, whom the child had said was her therapist. It seemed that the teacher had entered into a competition with the therapist, to be especially kind and understanding, to be the kind of person who accepted the child's bad feelings and alongside this the child's version of the very bad, harsh therapist, and had contributed to the child's splitting between the all-good teacher and the all-bad therapist. The rivalry to be the therapist was more directly expressed here than in earlier examples where the conflict was between the separate good things offered by teacher and therapist.

Labelling

In contrast to the aims and processes of therapy, it might seem easier to communicate the results of intelligence tests, and sometimes it is. It is likely to be work that the psychologist has carried out personally and the relevance of the results for school performance will be fairly well understood. When these results differ markedly, however, from the teacher's view of a child it is possible to get caught up in an empty argument as to who is right. Since both must, in some sense, be right, the alternative is to look together for the reasons for the discrepancy. This is, after all, impinging on the teacher's own area of expertise and may be a point, therefore, when the psychologist can most seem to challenge the teacher's skills. Where the results suggest the possibility of better functioning than has so far been achieved, then it can arouse feelings of failure, even of anger either with the child or the psychologist.

One way of easing everybody's distress has been by labelling the child as ESN, dyslexic, retarded or maladjusted and so on. Psychologists have been particularly liable to use this way out. Such labels can be used to write children off, as well as, more appropriately, to relieve a self-critical teacher.

Sue was a 10-year-old, nearly due for transfer to secondary school. She came from a very loving home and was mature and confident in spite of rather modest school achievements. The teachers, in her excellent primary school, had helped her considerably in her development, but now were worried about how she would manage in a secondary school. Her test results showed an IQ level not much over 70 which confirmed the cause for concern, being consistent with an ESN level of functioning. The tests also confirmed how well she had been helped by her school and home. In this case it was then possible to make an appropriate decision together with the family.

Harry was a very intelligent child, with a minor physical handicap, who began to have work difficulties after transfer to secondary school. It would have been easy to insist to the school that his test results were high, potentially up to a good academic standard, and that the good junior school performance had not been misleading. This could have prompted the school either into disbelief, or into a sense of failure. To emphasise the physical disability on the other hand would not have been fair to a boy who had tried hard to overcome it. Nevertheless this was the source of additional stress and fatigue. It was important not to label him handicapped which could also have raised the question of whether this was the right school for him, but instead to look in detail at the possible effects on his work. In the end quite modest allowances were necessary, and some counselling with the boy himself to understand and acknowledge the nature of his actual difficulties. A year later his report was considerably improved and no further intervention was necessary.

Of all labels, the psychiatric one can be the most frightening. Maurice's parents became fearful of this when his teachers, frustrated by his failure to learn to read, suggested referral to a Child Guidance Clinic. Ordinary remedial classes had not so far helped and the teacher felt there were underlying emotional problems. Instead of taking up the appointment offered at the clinic, Maurice's mother took him to another clinic and obtained a certificate of dyslexia. The diagnosis had been carefully made but later discussion with Maurice showed that he had interpreted the word to mean that he had a nasty, infectious illness and that his brain did not work properly. The sad effect was to make him feel at the mercy of his handicap, reduce his own feeling of control, and, as his teachers reported, seemed quite destructive of his efforts to learn to read.

Parents, school and clinic working together

Much of this chapter has highlighted the need not only for school and clinic to work together but for parents also to be included. This case illustrates one way in which this might be achieved.

The boy, Charles, had been assessed as subnormal many years

previously and was consequently attending a special school. As he was now 15 years old he was coming up to the point where a decision would have to be made about his future. He could, of course, leave school at 16, but it would also be possible for schooling to be extended, so he could stay on, but this had not yet been discussed. Instead the parents and the headmaster had been involved in a bitter debate revolving around the question of how effectively the school had managed to teach Charles so far. The parents were increasingly critical of what the school was offering and the school was responding by defending its record and insisting that it had not given up by writing Charles off.

The situation had become very bad and I suggested that we all meet together at school, with the headmaster, other relevant class teachers, the parents and myself. Listening to the heated exchanges it seemed to me that the parents were preparing the ground for withdrawing Charles as soon as he was 16, and the school was saying that there was really nothing more that could be done. When I drew attention to the fact that both parents and school seemed actually to want the same thing, that Charles should leave at 16 years, there was immediate relief. It then emerged that the school had been afraid of demands from the parents to keep Charles beyond 16 in order to teach him more, and the parents had interpreted the school's attitude as pressure for Charles to stay on, as he had not yet learned enough. There was laughter at the misperceptions on each side, and the parents then were able to acknowledge their more positive feelings about the school, since Charles had always been very happy there. In this atmosphere an agreed decision could be made for him to leave at 16. This seemed to be to everybody's satisfaction, including most importantly Charles himself.

Co-operation between teaching staff

There will be many occasions when the teachers in a school work together to solve their problems about a particular child, without a psychologist or any other outside advisor. By their very nature we do not generally hear about them, but some examples were described in the teachers' groups, and the following is an example of what is probably a fairly common situation.

Most pupils, especially in secondary schools, are in a web of relationships to a number of teachers, who are also, of course, in varying degrees of contact with each other. Felicity was the subject of concern to her biology teacher, Mrs S who was also head of the Human Science Department in a large comprehensive school. Most of the class were working with a reasonable prospect of success for the biology 'O' level examination. Felicity was being entered in spite of the fact that Mrs S thought she was likely to fail. Felicity was being seen on a regular basis by the school counsellor, who felt barred from discussing her with Mrs S because of possible breach of confidence. The teacher felt her relationship was worsened by an occasion when the head of the school had come into the classroom whilst Mrs S was briefly absent and had disciplined Felicity for disrupting the class. Felicity blamed her teacher for this. Felicity's year head was also a biology teacher and had been responsible for pressing for Felicity's inclusion in the class, in spite of Mrs S's doubts.

The different perspectives of the teachers concerned became clear to Mrs S as she described them. First, the counsellor, sympathetic to Felicity but bound by confidentiality and unable to explain the nature of her problems. Then the year head, keen to see her examination hopes for Felicity proved correct. Finally the head who was concerned about her disruptive behaviour in a generally fairly well-behaved class. Mrs S herself, felt rejected as a teacher by Felicity, in favour of the year head, whom Felicity preferred, and would work for. She also felt unable to enquire into Felicity's worries as that would cut across the role of the counsellor. In this unsatisfactory situation Mrs S fell back on trying to protect the work of her class against the bad influence of this one failing member.

Mrs S became clearer about her own feelings towards Felicity, her resentment that she had been imposed on her hard working class, and her wish that she could be removed. With this clearer perspective Mrs S was able to sort out a joint approach with the counsellor, which would reduce the split being created between them. Fortunately the two, teacher and counsellor, normally got on well together. Mrs S was also able to make a new work plan with the year head, which they could both agree, and which would allow for a subsequent clear decision as to whether or not Felicity should sit for the examination. The head was kept informed but was able to stand back whilst the staff had their discussions.

The school as mirrored in the classroom

An even more striking example of the way in which the organisation of the school as a whole can be reflected in an individual classroom was provided in the case of a well-established grammar school which was in the process of being transformed into a comprehensive catering for all levels of ability. Miss J described a new class in which classical history was being taught to a mixed group drawn from a number of classes. For most of the children the course was a less academic option than the normal course in classics, in which the grammar school had always excelled. One quite large group, however, joined, having for other reasons, got on badly in the usual classics class. Even though the new class had produced some interesting projects and seemed keen to succeed Miss J found them a very unhappy group, constantly at odds with each other, unfriendly and hostile. The school was particularly keen that this experimental lesson should succeed, and it seemed to have come to symbolise the efforts to integrate the best of the school's past into its new structure. Miss J noted that the children stayed in groups according to their original classes, but did not think that forcing them to mix would improve matters. In considering how the children had been selected and prepared for the new class she discovered that the teacher of the more able group was virtually alone amongst the staff in not approving of the experiment. It was this group which was especially troublesome, mocking and resentful of any success by the others, and clinging most strongly to a separate identity.

The struggles of the school as it tried to adapt to its new intake, to hold on to its good reputation, both for careful teaching and for a sympathetic approach to its pupils, and to agree on the best strategies, seemed to be especially reflected in this class as it became a focus for a new experiment, in many ways a copy in miniature of the wider experiment involving the whole school.

Looking at the problems in this classroom provided a way of looking at some of the issues in the school as a whole. The unanimous wish of the staff group to make a success of the change to comprehensive, and the skilful guidance of a headmistress who kept an open dialogue with her staff, allowed the debate about the wider issues to be continued in the staffroom. For Miss J the episode remained an example of how the morale and relationships, and the very structure of the school can appear in the apparently independent sub-unit of the classroom and become the responsibility of the individual teacher.

Part V

Endings

I. Salzberger-Wittenberg

Chapter 10

Different kinds of endings

Introduction

The end of term, the end of a school year; the temporary or permanent
end of an important relationship, the end of school, childhood, youth;
bereavement and the end of our life – all these situations in varying
degrees confront us with the experience of loss. We have to come to terms
with losing what has sustained and supported us and those whom we have
needed, loved and depended on. Will we be able to manage without the
presence of parent, friend, partner, mentor? Have they abandoned us to
our fate, left us to die, to feel lonely and bereft? Will they come back
again, or will ill befall them in our absence? Will they remember us? Can
we give up our demand that they be available to us endlessly? Can we
cherish their memory and what they gave us? Can we let go of the comfort
and privileges of babyhood, childhood, youth – of life itself, without too
much resentment? Even a conflict-laden situation may be hard to part
from for it offers some sense of security by being familiar. We may in
addition dread what might take its place; as the saying goes: 'better the
devil you know than the one you don't know.' It is only if the past or
present is disastrous that we contemplate the end with sheer relief.

We shall examine some of the ordinary ending situations in the lives of
students and teachers. The anxieties and pain which accompany such
situations are rarely faced, yet how these experiences are dealt with is of
great importance in determining what of the past can be retained and used
creatively in the present and future.

Transfer to another teacher

In most schools, children experience frequent staff changes. They are
passed regularly from one teacher to another as lessons follow each other

during the course of a day. Supply and student teachers appear for a limited time and on an irregular basis; in addition there may be a considerable staff turn-over due to change of job, marriage or promotion.

Yet such temporary or permanent changes are rarely talked about. At best they are mentioned by the by, but the feelings evoked by such comings and goings are generally not faced. It took me some years of teaching on the course for teachers at the Tavistock to fully realise that even a temporary hand-over of the large group to another staff member caused considerable disruption. I had noticed on a number of occasions that the colleague who took over for a few meetings was given a hard time. He/she noticed that the group was disturbed by the change and I was aware upon my return how hard it was to resume the relationship with the members of the group. Sometimes I was welcomed back enthusiastically and my colleague talked about rather disparagingly as a supply teacher, or else the group tended to get highly excited about the new teacher, as if all their good feelings were now invested in him/her and our past relationship forgotten. While some change and variety are no doubt enriching, any change involves some degree of anxiety. It seemed to me that here we had a chance to explore at first hand the emotional factors involved in a transfer to another teacher; to study a phenomenon which continually occurs in all educational institutions, without much attention paid to what these changes mean to students. The following comments were made by members when we were discussing the fact that a colleague of mine would be teaching the group for three weeks. I have sorted them under headings which indicate the general attitude to the change, but the remarks came roughly in the order indicated:

(a) Fear of loss of holding situation:

'Oh dear, we'll have to start right from the beginning again and go back to all the chaos.'

'It will be strange for you not to be here, we've got used to you now and that feels safe.'

'When you go away it is as if a link gets broken.'

'You hold the memory of the group.'

(b) Anger with the person leaving:

'You are deserting us.'

'You don't seem to care about us, you just pick us up and put us down.'

'We might just as well not have got started with you.'

'Mrs W – Oh, I have forgotten your full name already.'

'I'm not going to attend when that other person comes.'

(c) Denigration of the old relationship and idealisation of the new one:

'I didn't like the way you handled the group.'

'I like changes, anyway it will be nice to have a more friendly teacher.'

'I'm not sure how useful these meetings have been.'

'Maybe the new teacher will be better.'

'You made us work hard, it will be nice to have a rest.'

'Maybe she'll supply some answers instead of raising so many questions – it'll be much easier.'

'It will be a pleasant change, it gets boring having the same person all the time.'

'I hope she'll use some visual aids, it'll be more fun.'

(d) Phantasies about the cause for teacher's leaving:

'You've been looking tired, perhaps you are not well and need a rest.'

'Maybe you got fed up with us and can't stand us any more.'

'Perhaps you don't like us and prefer another group.'

'I suppose you have better things to do than teaching us.'

(e) Attempts to preserve good feelings:

'In any case you're coming back in three week's time, it's not a long absence.'

'I'm sad to see you go, we shall miss you.'

'I've enjoyed the course so far.'

'I'm sure you care enough to find a good person to take the group over.'

'I've learnt so much from these meetings, they have really taught me something I shall remember.'

Conflicting emotions at separation

These quotations give some indication of the conflicting emotions aroused by a separation, however temporary. It may seem surprising that a teacher's absence can evoke such powerful feelings. The poignancy of the situation lies in the function which the teacher fulfils for the group (and the individuals within it) and the anxieties stirred up in the depth of the mind. For any separation evokes earlier situations of being left by mother and father, and thus the fear of being once again exposed to feeling helpless, in a state of chaos and panic. By nature of his role and/or personality the teacher may therefore be experienced as the person who holds the different parts of the mentality of each individual within the group as well as holding together in his mind the different aspects of the members which comprise the group. Without his containing presence, the group fears that it will fall apart, be lost, lose the link between its component parts and in addition lose the memory of the past good experiences. Such anxieties cause anger with the person who is felt to be responsible for putting individuals into such a predicament. In turn, destructive feelings contribute to the anxiety that any good gained in the relationship will be lost forever. For the anger and fear of experiencing the pain of losing someone of importance makes individuals devalue the present, treat the loss as a good riddance, turn their backs on it, and quickly replace it with what is hoped to be a more ideal relationship with a new teacher.

The ability to bear loss will be influenced by how successfully previous experiences of separation and loss in childhood have been negotiated; in particular the experience of being weaned from the breast or the feeding mother. This will depend partly on the child's ability to bear frustration without too much resentment. All separation involves some frustration, anger and anxiety. It is of the utmost importance whether the result of such emotional pains is an avoidance and expulsion, or alternatively a modulation of the pain through the mental work of thinking and remembering. When destructive feelings predominate, the baby/pupil/group is left not simply with an absent mother/parent/teacher, but the pervasive internal presence of a bad one: the nasty, deserting, uncaring or punitive one. This will affect not only his relationship with the one who has left, but adversely his ability to hold on to and use what he has received and learnt from it. While the loved one is absent, some temporary substitute may be essential to keep going; thus a baby finds his thumb, a child a toy, an adult another person, while he is awaiting the return of the one he depends on. Some infants and children, however, come to prefer some inanimate object that is constantly available and thus under their control to a relationship with an alive (and hence coming and going) person.

Weaning is the first experience of permanent loss. Some infants are so disappointed and angry when they are weaned that they turn with hatred against the mother and invest the relationship to the father with idealised hope. The capacity to mourn is highly dependent on the mother's ability to handle separations with care and wean the baby gently, furthermore on her capacity to bear the inevitable feelings of anger, guilt and sadness. Yet because of her own feelings of guilt or depression, she may (just like the teacher) be emotionally absent and even physically withdrawn. This is bound to make the baby feel more rejected and anxious that she is unwilling or unable to care for him. Indeed, at such a time, babies need extra attention and loving. Some mothers, unable to bear sadness, try to jolly the baby out of this painful state. This conveys the idea that such feelings are unbearable; they can therefore not be worked through. At later times of loss the individual will then not have had experiences of sadness forming a valuable basis for yearning and keeping alive the memory of the good missing person.

Part of the anxiety experienced by the individual relates to phantasies about the reasons for the loss. They may be of a persecutory nature, e.g. fearing that the teacher is punishing them, or that he dislikes and rejects the group, just as the child feels unwanted and unloved by the parent who goes away. They may be of a more depressive nature, concerned with having exhausted the teacher's strength and/or tolerance, evoking earlier feelings of having emptied or damaged the breast, or tired out his parents. In addition there will be all sorts of ideas about what the teacher may be doing when he is absenting himself from the group. The feelings of rivalry and envy arising from such phantasies may further contribute to the anger with the teacher.

All these emotions are likely to be evoked to some extent at a separation from a person who holds an important position in the students' minds. If the teacher can allow the anger to be expressed in his presence, it makes it possible for the students to see that he can survive such onslaught and yet remain loving and caring. This gives a chance for phantasies of a rejecting, nasty or weak teacher to be compared to the reality. Such good memories may then be put against the anxieties and phantasies that arise during the teacher's absence. It also allows for more positive and reparative feelings to come to the fore while the teacher is still present, and thus it may be possible to part on better terms. Teachers often find it just as difficult to accept the expression of sadness and affection as they do the more hostile feelings. It is rare for a teacher to actually be able to share sadness and pain at parting. He might, however, take care to pay more attention to the pupil's wish to show appreciation and his need to be remembered. This may take the form of giving the teacher a personal gift, e.g. a poem, a painting or a piece of handicraft. This is to be distinguished from the abundance of insincere compliments, showers of presents and shows of gratitude which characterise most leaving-parties.

In view of the painful emotions aroused by partings, it is hardly surprising that most teachers simply avoid thinking about the subject. Instead they feel surprised and hurt if the group is hostile and tending to turn away from them even before they have left. At some level teachers are well aware of the pain that they inflict by leaving and, as a result, feel too guilty to be able to fully face the situation with the group or with individual children; they simply bow out. It may take several weeks for a group to get over a temporary break, while permanent partings need months of preparation. Otherwise the new teacher may carry the unfair burden of being the recipient of all the resentment which the students have been unable to express to the teacher who has left. Often the teacher feels the loss as acutely as the students. This is especially so for teachers to whom the class represents an alternative to a family. Feelings of possessiveness – 'my children', 'my class', may make it very hard to face the handing over of a class to another teacher. Some teachers fear that the new teacher will be better, the children will become more attached to him/her, and not wish to see the old one back. Furthermore, there may be an anxiety that one will be adversely judged by the replacement-teacher in terms of the curriculum covered, the standard of performance and behaviour of the class. Such feelings of rivalry, persecution and depression in the teacher may add to the difficulty of discussing and accepting the feelings of the students. But avoiding talking about the separation, even a temporary one, does not mean the experience is forgotten. On the contrary, the student may experience the teacher as simply not caring or else too weak or frightened to face the painful feelings of anger and depression involved. Moreover, if the teacher is seen not to have the courage to bear such feelings, then it becomes doubly hard for the student to do so.

If losses are felt to be too painful, the individual may fear to attach himself to any one person deeply, and thus his relationships tend to become superficial. When there have been many losses in a person's life, it may be thought to be too risky to form any deep attachments again. Such a situation pertains with children who are moved about a great deal, from school to school, place to place, from country to country. Often such pupils are basically depressed, having been unable to deal with repeated unworked-over losses. Aware of the pain of separation, some teachers feel that they should not get involved with a child who is only in their care for a short time. This is a mistaken view for the contact with an understanding and sympathetic adult will help to raise hope that such relationships exist, while a superficial approach leads to further despair that there is nobody who is capable of caring. It is, however, essential that we prepare students for our (or their) leaving, rather than abandon them suddenly, thus showing that we are concerned enough to think about the continuity of the life of the student beyond the span of our external presence. When parents take their children out of school and transfer them to another, it will be of great importance for the children to have the opportunity to say goodbye to their friends and teachers and part amicably. This is so even when the child has been absent for some time or the parents have every reason to be dissatisfied with the school. Without proper leave-taking, no ending can be experienced, and a new situation is then entered into with unfinished business that can never be completed. If parting can be accomplished without either angry obliteration of what is past, or denial of the ending, there is less actual loss – for the goodness of the relationship can be kept in mind and thus live on internally, remaining as a source of strength.

Holidays

For most teachers holidays come as a welcome relief from hard work and a rigorous timetable. A period of rest, relaxation, change and recreation are essential. We tend to assume that this applies in equal measure to our students. This may be so to quite some extent, especially for the older ones, and those whose home and leisure time offer positive alternatives to school life. But our too ready assumption of the benefit of holidays may make it difficult to recognise that the end of term is also often fraught with anxiety, anger and depression. Let us look a little more closely at what the end of term means to the child-like parts of the personality.

Breaking up

It is significant that this is the expression used when referring to the end of term. When we looked at a particular teacher leaving a class, we noted how this was felt as his breaking the link with the class. At depth the teacher is experienced as a parental figure who provides and cares, holds the group in his mind, and his disappearance threatens to break this life-line. When the whole of the teaching staff and student-body go away and the premises close down, even more anxiety may be provoked. The whole institution is then unavailable, evoking all the deeper fears that the fabric of home, family, parents, and siblings can disappear, leaving the children lost in the big wide world without external support. In addition, there is the removal of structure. Although adherence to rules of behaviour, the regularity imposed by a timetable and prescribed tasks may be resented, their absence may leave the child, and the child within the adult, bewildered, afraid of a freedom which exposes them to facing the emptiness and chaos of their internal world.

Excitement and depression

Work is often abandoned well before the end of term, with plans and preparation for the holidays the main focus of preoccupation. This tends to be particularly the case before Christmas. Lights and decorations engender excitement, special foods of the season stimulate oral cravings, while presents expected or asked for are often invested with an exaggerated hope of bringing happiness. Such expectations are by the more mature known to be only skin-deep and their place is taken by a deep longing for unity, harmony, beauty and peace within one's own family and amongst the family of nations. The story of Christmas, as well as that of other religions, have as their central theme the triumph of hope over despair, good over evil, light over darkness, peace over disharmony. Religious beliefs can help to sustain such hopes and the determination to strive after ideals; but in as far as these ideals remain unfulfilled, this may serve to only cast a deeper shadow over the reality of our existence; not only do presents fail to bring the fulfilment of our wishes, but the disharmony of the family or its incompleteness (through separation, divorce, childlessness, death) is likely just at this time to be very acutely felt and engender deep feelings of depression. Comparisons abound, both before and during the holiday, with the conviction that others have more in the way of material comforts, affection, love or harmonious relationships. This makes it so difficult to describe the holiday afterwards to others in anything but the most glowing terms; it is so hard to admit that the holiday has been disappointing or brought unhappiness. Children not only compare their presents and home-life amongst themselves, but have phantasies about the teacher and his/her family. That the teacher has a life apart from the school may of course be totally denied; as one child put it – 'you are just like a puppet in the cupboard who is taken out by the headmaster after the holiday to teach us.' But in as far as the pupil can allow himself to think of the teacher as having a life of his own, he may feel jealous of the teacher's family who is getting the attention and care that he would like to have for himself. The student may fear to be deserted, forgotten about by both the teacher and his peers. Hence the scratching of names into desks and chairs, inscribing of walls in indelible ink, the exchange of sweaters and similar behaviour. Some children, unable to face endings, drift away, absent themselves from school for the last few days or even weeks. Some give expression to their sense of lostness by wandering about the streets aimlessly, while others become so depressed that they may take to staying in bed.

Destructive behaviour

While some children react to holidays by becoming withdrawn and depressed, others are unable to contain within their minds depression and loss – instead they enact the experience of breaking apart and chaos. This may result in very uncontrolled behaviour like throwing flour and eggs, pulling out and setting off fire extinguishers, smashing tables and chairs or throwing equipment through the window. While this may represent the feeling that the structure of the school is disintegrating, it can also be the result of jealousy and envy. It is as if the pupils were saying: 'If we cannot enjoy the good things the school and the teachers can offer, then we shall spoil it so that no-one can have it.' Sometimes such behaviour is mistakenly attributed to a sense of freedom and relief at the absence of rules and regulations. It is more likely that such pupils will become frightened at the damage wrought and fearful of having to return to it after the holiday. Such a pupil also takes away within his mind the image of hurt teachers, thus leaving him without the inner support of mentors who provide structure and meaningfulness in his life. One teacher described how the boys in school cut each others' ties, while the girls stand around screaming and crying. We might say that such behaviour could be understood literally to mean that a child experiences the tie to be cut by the teacher (like an umbilical cord) but prefers to be the active agent in this process. It is felt to be a cruel ending rather than a gentle putting down. It would seem that the girls' behaviour expresses excitement, horror and fright at the boys' triumphant assertion that they can now manage on their own and do not need ties of affection, dependency or controls of any kind.

In this situation it is the teacher who is likely to be left feeling rejected, unloved, uncared for and despairing. When teachers react with fear and withdrawal, they will be experienced as actually having been smashed, while if they become punitive, the children may feel their own behaviour to be justified and lose any sense of their cruelty. Many schools, as if to counteract the fear of disintegration and disharmony, engage in some activity intended to bring the school together as a united whole. This may take the form of a concert, play, exhibition of work, or some other kind of celebration. While this might to some extent be a papering over of underlying cracks and conflicts, it is an important demonstration of the fact that the school is *not* falling apart, but able to survive and maintain a structure which can contain the conflicting parts within it and remain a working unit. There are many ways in which children try to maintain concrete links with the school, like taking drawings and other evidence of their achievements home, or looking after a school pet. All these may help to keep the memory of school and their good relationships they have established there alive over the holiday.

Post-holiday behaviour and feelings

The way in which students return from holiday depends in part on the mental state in which they left and the feelings carried over from before the holiday. Here is an example from the teachers' group. There was a heavy snowfall on the evening that we reassembled for the spring term. Attendance was low and those who had come wondered what had happened to the rest of the group. Had the snow prevented them from coming? Had something untoward happened to them? Were they simply not coming back because they did not want to continue? I was struck by the fact that everyone had taken it for granted that I would be there – yet I had only just managed to get to the meeting. Someone jokingly said: 'Surely, you are at this place all the time.'

One is impressed how, at one level, we all think like children. It reminded us of pupils who believe the teacher lives at school and of younger ones who have the notion that the teacher stays put in the same classroom, eating and sleeping there, totally boxed in and cut off from any outside contact. This preserves a sense of security, and protects one from the anxiety of not being able to find the teacher when one wants him, and having to worry about his safety. Such a belief also saves one from feelings of jealousy and envy in relation to the teacher's family and out-of-school activities.

Someone remembered that there had been a very heated discussion on the last occasion we had met. We had reviewed the course and some strong criticism had been voiced. Those who had felt more positive felt guilty that they hadn't spoken up in defence of the course. They said that they had not done so because they did not wish to be rude to each other, and upset other members who might be too fragile to stand disagreement. In spite of this it would seem that in their minds, i.e. in phantasy, both the staff and other members were experienced as having been harmed. This experience has taught me that review meetings should not be held on the last evening of term: having it earlier enables explosive feelings to be expressed, and yet have the chance to check that such onslaught has done no permanent damage to the relationship. Meeting again may also provide an opportunity for more thoughtfulness as well as reparation to those who have been hurt. The anxiety in the group on this occasion was considerable, and this was shown by the behaviour of some of the members: one teacher had last week on his way home 'looked in to make sure that the building was still there,' while two others had come to check whether the staff were around. Others stayed away for the first week, needing to be invited back as if to make sure that they were still welcome.

When students show reluctance to settle down after a holiday, it is generally assumed that they resent getting back to work. While this may be to some extent correct, we can see from the above example that the survival of the school, the teacher, the peer-group *and* learning comes as a great relief. Difficulties in coming back are often related to resentment and anxiety about the teacher's absence, to the fear of being unwanted, unloved, and the dread of the reparative work that may have to be done as a result of destructive actions and phantasies. It is important for the teacher to show that the students have been kept in mind, e.g. by remembering what occurred before the holiday and caring about what happened to them during the holiday. This will be part of gathering them back, making it easier to re-establish a friendly relationship and settle down to the new term's activities.

The end of a course of education

We face many endings and transitions during our progress through the educational system: the end of the year, the end of infant, primary, secondary school – and perhaps a period of higher education, trade or professional training. Each ending means leave-taking, looking back over the past and forward to the future. It brings with it loss of the friends and teachers as well as the loss of the institution that we have known and the support we have received. Frequently, a group makes arrangements to go on meeting but, while reunions may be enjoyable, we tend to fool ourselves into believing that relationships will be the same as before. On the other hand, children and older students often like to re-visit the school or college at least once to reassure themselves of its continued existence and to feel that they are still welcome.

Each step forward on the educational ladder means more independence and freedom from some restrictions, yet it also brings with it the loss of childhood or student-hood, a period of relative freedom and security which will be replaced by one which involves having to take on a greater degree of responsibility. Transitions of this kind lead us to take stock of where we have got to, what we have achieved or failed to achieve, what we have made of the experience that is coming to an end and how well we are equipped to enter the next stage of our life. We may look back with satisfaction, be filled with pleasure, pride and relief at having stayed the course, reached a certain standard, obtained recognition. We may be eager to prove that we are now capable of putting into practice what we have learnt. At the same time, the anxiety and negative feelings stimulated by the knowledge of ending can be so powerful that they have the effect of bringing about a premature end to learning. This may be shown by increased absenteeism, with various excuses like end-of-year activities, preparation for examinations or job hunting.

Even when students are there in body, their minds may be closed off. As one student expressed it: 'I stopped learning last term because it's too late now anyway,' and another said: 'If the course is going to stop, it will be less painful to start cutting myself off now.' Such feeling of despair, or an attempt to avoid pain at something alive and valuable coming to an end, means that there is an actual loss of learning. These experiences have led me to discuss the ending of the course at the beginning of the last term, in the hope that this will be conducive to keeping working and learning vibrant right up to the end. I shall now describe some of the feelings that have been voiced and are generally experienced (though often not consciously) by students as they approach the end of the course.

The students' feelings at ending

Loss of opportunity

'I have just become aware that I'll never have a chance like this again.'

'I haven't appreciated until now the freedom that we have had to study and think.'

'I am aware that I haven't used the teachers as much as I could – I have always been afraid to show my weaknesses and yet I could have got so

149

much more help if I had been more open about them.'

'I have wasted a lot of time just trying to get by with a minimum.'

'There are so many things I have never understood and I didn't bother to ask about.'

'I fear I haven't made my mark, and hence will be forgotten.'

'I feel I will leave a bad impression behind – I don't know whether I can still redeem it.'

Such realisations lead to sadness and regret out of which may grow a more acute awareness of the limited time there is left. This may result in increased learning and harder work, trying to make up for wasted time and opportunities, so that the last few months may be marked by greater effort and a spurt in learning.

Doubts and worries about one's adequacy

Those students who are doing poorly are bound to feel doubtful about their ability to face the greater demands that will be made on them in the future, whether this be by another teacher, a higher class, a higher school, a further course of education, or a job. Such students may show considerable anxiety or depression and require the transition to be discussed and handled with care by the teacher. Others deal with their lack of progress by denying any difficulties in themselves and believing that it is the school and teachers who are holding them back. Many adolescents seem hardly able to wait to leave what they experience as unjustifiable restrictions and infantilisation. Yet quite a few of these same adolescents come back to their school teacher and seek reassurance and comfort from him once they have had a taste of the demands made on them by their employers and the world of work. Even those who are doing well at school or a course, and are accorded praise and given written evidence of their achievements, are likely to have doubts about how much they have learnt. Here are some quotations of comments made:

'I am not sure what I have learnt, I shall not know until it is put to the test.'

'I don't know whether I have learnt enough to be sufficiently well equipped for the job.'

'How will I manage in the future without support?'

'I am not at all sure whether I will remember anything I have learnt.'

'I don't know whether I can build on what I have learnt and develop further when there is no one to keep an eye on me and encourage me.'

It is indeed very difficult to be sure about what learning has taken place unless there is a clear-cut skill which can be demonstrated. Such doubts beset any thoughtful student and those who do not voice unease may be the ones to worry about. In as far as their apparent over-confidence is based on denial and omnipotence, this may suddenly collapse and they may then find themselves overwhelmed by anxiety and unable to face examinations.

What is being put to the test at separation and afterwards are the following:

(a) how much has been truly learnt, i.e. become part and parcel of the student's mental and emotional equipment. In as far as the student has simply made progress on the basis of imitation or living on and through the teacher, there is very little that the student is able to take away with him;

(b) how angry the student is at the absence of the teacher; or alternatively how grateful for the help he has received, and hence wanting to preserve what he has learnt, and go on struggling, seeking help only when necessary. Those unable to retain knowledge and take the responsibility for their own further learning, tend to want to cling on to their past tutors, assure themselves that help will still be available to them or register for a new course before the present one has finished. Some of these become eternal students;

(c) how much responsibility the student can take for his own development. In as far as the student is relying purely on the attention and encouragement of his teacher in order to maintain his interest and progress in a subject, he will find it hard to continue learning when he is on his own.

Jealousy and envy

Those who are leaving friends, an admired teacher or a prestigious institution, may feel jealous of the next year's students who are going to take their place. They are experienced as younger siblings, mother's and father's new baby and envied for what they will get. Often it is feared that the new student (baby) will be nicer and better than oneself and hence preferred. He may even be felt to have an advantage because the teacher has gained in experience and hence may have become better at his job. Such feelings can make students feel reluctant to discuss how a course might be improved in the future, resentful that others rather than themselves will benefit. Sometimes this leads to suggestions that conditions and standards should be more stringent, making it harder for those who come after them!

There may be envy of those who remain behind and can still use each other for support. Such feelings apply both to on-going student groups and to the staff group. Often there is envy of the teacher who, as the owner of knowledge and skill and wisdom, will go on profiting from such possessions. He may even be suspected of having deliberately given only a little of what he has to offer so as to keep the rest to himself.

The teacher's feelings at ending

The student's attitude to the ending of the contact and the anxieties aroused are matched to some extent by those of teachers.

Loss of opportunity

A caring teacher will ask himself, 'Have I done enough for this group and for each one of the students within it; have I tried hard enough to further the student's capacities; have I applied myself sufficiently to find a way to teach him; have I given of my best or done only a minimum?' There may be guilt, especially as regards those who have failed, have not profited enough or not reached their potential. This will be felt in relation to their practical and academic achievement; in addition many teachers will ask themselves whether they have made enough of the chance to help the students' emotional development, aware of their great responsibility to further or hinder it. Not only will they consider whether they have cared enough about them, but also whether they have helped them to gain enough responsibility and self-reliance to stand on their own feet.

Fear of wasted effort

Where the teacher has invested a great deal of attention and care, he may wonder anxiously: will it all be wasted and thrown away? He finds himself in a position similar to parents whose adolescents, on the brink of leaving home, show little evidence of having imbibed love and care but instead behave carelessly and callously in relation to themselves and others. As regards academic achievement, the fact that examination results are usually known only after the end of the year, means that failure may never be fully faced. The student may thus feel abandoned rather than sustained in his plight. Nor is he given help in making realistic alternative plans; thorough and constructive career guidance is very rarely provided.

Teachers may also feel that the environment in which the student will find himself after leaving school or course, will undermine what he has learnt in the past: they may be concerned about the lack of employment opportunity and work satisfaction for the student whom they have so carefully nurtured. Like parents, teachers ask themselves whether they have prepared their pupils for the real world or cossetted them too much, given them a sense of responsibility or made them too dependent to manage on their own.

Jealousy and envy

Teachers are sometimes jealous of the on-going relationships between members of a group who are continuing together. They may also be jealous of the positive attachment which students might develop to the teacher who takes them on. Some teachers envy the opportunity of the young for further learning and work opportunities, particularly where these exceed those that existed when they were young themselves. The youngsters going out into the world may be envied for the possibilities of development and success that lie in front of them, especially when the teacher feels that his own chance of advancement is limited.

Loss of a relationship

Most teachers become attached to the groups they teach as well as to individual students. Teachers, too, may therefore experience the end of the relationship as painful. Students on our courses are usually surprised and pleased to hear that we shall miss them, that we are concerned about their future and interested to hear how they fare. Moreover, as teachers, we have got to know and found a way of working with individuals and groups and may dread having to start all over again with another intake. Unless these issues are faced and some mourning takes place, new students might find themselves the recipients of anger and depression simply because they are different from the old group and the teacher is reluctant to start afresh. These matters are barely thought about and practically never acknowledged by staff-groups and institutions. Instead they deny that a relationship is ending, collude with absenteeism, behave as if, once exams are over, the term has really come to an end, and allow relationships to fizzle out. They make little effort to hold on to the group because of their fear of their own, as well as their students', sadness. The painful feelings are literally run away from by engaging in boisterous activities like sports, or drowned by the laughter, food and drink at leaving-parties.

Retaining something of value

As external relationships come to a temporary or permanent end, the fear that one will forget as well as be forgotten and lose what has been of value, assumes paramount importance. Such anxiety makes students and teachers alike look for proofs of achievement and wish to embody it in something concrete. Children, anxious that their contributions and their knowledge will be lost, like to take home and safeguard their drawings, carpentry, sculptures, as well as school books at the end of each year. For students, pieces of paper declaring that they have reached a certain standard assume great importance. They are carefully wrapped up and kept, prizes are framed and displayed, and school photographs become a permanent memento of past relationships. At the end of the year the staff of the educational institution are keen to invite outsiders to share and admire exhibitions, school or college performances and to participate in prize-givings. Such experiences serve to reassure everyone within the institution that their efforts have been worthwhile. 'A good end' helps both students and staff to retain a memory of a past they can be proud of. There is another reason why it may be important to bring the families of the students into a leaving ceremony; having participated or witnessed it, they are able to help the individual leaver to retain the memory of the institution and the people within it.

While all these factors may play some part in helping one's memory, they are no more than aids in trying to preserve internally what has been of value in one's past experience. If we can be grateful for what we have received and remember our mentors with more love than anger, with more gratitude than grudge, then we will be able to hold on permanently to something of the goodness gained in those relationships. It implies that the past is not obliterated, nor the loss denied. It involves us in some sadness and missing what we have had, and yet, out of appreciation, endeavouring to keep it alive in our minds. The past can never be ignored or undone. We can try to kill it off inside ourselves but by doing so we cut ourselves off from our roots and parts of ourselves. We then feel insecure and have no inner store on which to base our future.

Alternatively, if we can preserve the externally lost relationship within our minds, we are able to build on the inner groundwork we have developed, and feel we have some internal resources with which to face the future hopefully. This makes it possible to enter a new relationship without denying or smashing up the past, but rather by transferring the good feelings from the past and the hope gained thereby to the new situation. The fact that any relationship and life itself is not infinite, can make us more appreciative of what is available to us, for however limited a time, and have more regard for its preciousness. Such appreciation and gratitude for what we have received may lead to a wish to contribute to the life of others and in this way hand on and further develop the work of our teachers. This becomes the basis and the mainspring for reparative and creative work.

Further reading

If you would like to pursue your interest in the subjects discussed, the following books are suggested as a starting point:

BION, Wilfred R., *Experiences in Groups*, Tavistock Publications, 1961.
CASPARI, Irene, *Troublesome Children in Class*, Routledge & Kegan Paul, 1976.
GOODACRE, Elizabeth J., *School and Home*, National Foundation for Educational Research, 1970.
HARRIS, Martha, *Thinking about Infants and Young Children*, Clunie Press, 1975.
KLEIN, Melanie, *The Writings of Melanie Klein*, Vol. I: *Love, Guilt and Reparation* (1937), Vol. II: *Our Adult World and Its Roots in Infancy* (1959), Hogarth Press and the Institute of Psychoanalysis, 1975.
MONEY-KYRLE, Roger E., *Man's Picture of his World*, Duckworth, 1961.
SALZBERGER-WITTENBERG, Isca, *Psycho-Analytic Insight and Relationships*, Routledge & Kegan Paul, 1970.
WINNICOTT, Donald W., *The Child, the Family and the Outside World*, Penguin, 1964.